NUTSHELLS

CONTRACT

IN A

NUTSHELL

AUSTRALIA
Law Book Company
Sydney

CANADA and USA
Carswell
Toronto

HONG KONG
Sweet & Maxwell Asia

NEW ZEALAND
Brookers
Wellington

SINGAPORE and MALAYSIA
Sweet & Maxwell Asia
Singapore and Kuala Lumpur

NUTSHELLS

CONTRACT
IN A
NUTSHELL

SEVENTH EDITION

by

Robert Duxbury, LL.B. Barrister,
Principal Lecturer in Law,
Nottingham Law School,
Nottingham Trent University

London • Sweet & Maxwell • 2006

Published in 2006 by Sweet & Maxwell Limited of
100 Avenue Road, London, NW3 3PF
Typeset by LBJ Typesetting Ltd of Kingsclere
Printed in Wales by Creative Print and Design Group

No natural forests were destroyed to make this product.
Only farmed timber was used and re-planted.

A CIP catalogue record for this book is available
from the British Library.

ISBN 0 421 924 101

©
Sweet & Maxwell
2006

CONTENTS

CONTENTS

1. INTRODUCTION

DEFINITION OF CONTRACT

A contract may be defined as an agreement between two or more parties that is binding in law. This means that the agreement generates rights and obligations that may be enforced in the courts. The normal method of enforcement is an action for damages for breach of contract, though in some cases the court may compel performance by the party in default.

CLASSIFICATION OF CONTRACTS

The traditional classification of contracts is divided into "contracts by deed" and "simple contracts".

Contracts by deed

The contract is of ancient origin and derives its validity from the form in which it is made. It must be in writing and must be signed, witnessed, and delivered. Promises made by deed do not need to be supported by consideration (see Chapter 4) in order to be enforceable.

Simple contracts

All other contracts may be classified as simple contracts, whether they are made in writing, orally or by conduct. The law of simple contracts is the subject-matter of this book.

Another way of classifying contracts is according to whether they are "bilateral" or "unilateral".

Bilateral contracts

Here a promise by one party is exchanged for a promise by the other. The exchange of the promises is enough to render them both enforceable; thus, in a contract for the sale of goods, the buyer promises to pay the price and the seller promises to deliver the goods.

Unilateral contracts

Here one party promises to do something in return for an act of the other party, as opposed to a promise, e.g. where A promises a reward to anyone who will find his lost wallet. The essence of the unilateral contract is that only one party, A, is bound to do anything. No one is bound to search for the lost wallet, but if B, having seen the offer, recovers the wallet and returns it, he is entitled to the reward. (Unilateral contracts are discussed in Chapter 2.)

ELEMENTS OF THE LAW OF CONTRACT

There are three basic elements in the formation of a valid simple contract. First, the parties must have reached agreement (offer and acceptance); secondly, they must intend to be legally bound; and thirdly, both parties must have provided valuable consideration. These matters are dealt with in Chapters 2–4.

In addition, the parties must have the legal capacity to contract, and, in some cases, there must be compliance with certain formalities (see Chapter 5).

A contract consists of various terms, both express and implied. A term may be inserted into the contract to exclude or restrict one party's liability (see Chapters 6 and 7).

A contract may be invalidated by a mistake, or by illegality (see Chapters 9 and 11), and where the contract has been induced by misrepresentation, duress or undue influence, the innocent party may have the right to set it aside (see Chapters 8 and 10).

At common law, third parties had no rights under a contract but this rule is subject to many exceptions and has been substantially modified by recent legislation (see Chapter 12). The discharge of contracts and the remedies available are dealt with in Chapters 13 and 14.

2. OFFER AND ACCEPTANCE

If a contract is a legally binding agreement, the first question to consider is the method by which the courts ascertain whether a contract has been formed. Formerly, the courts were concerned with whether there had been a meeting of the minds of the two parties, or *consensus ad idem*. The approach is now objective, i.e. would a reasonable observer assume an agreement to have been concluded on certain terms. The conventional formula for this is to consider whether one party (the offeror) has made an offer which has been accepted by the other (the offeree) so as to conclude a contract. The objective approach is illustrated by *Moran v University College Salford (No.2)*, CA, 1996, where a university applicant was made an unconditional offer of a place in error. It was held that the claimant's acceptance concluded a binding contract despite the error, of which the claimant was unaware. Offer and acceptance will now be considered in turn.

OFFER

An offer may be defined as a statement of willingness to contract on specified terms made with the intention that, if accepted, it shall become a binding contract. An offer may be express or implied from conduct. It may be addressed to one particular person, a group of persons, or the world at large, as in an offer of a reward. Thus, in *Carlill v Carbolic Smoke Ball Co.* CA, 1893, the defendants advertised that they would pay £100 to anyone who contracted influenza after using their smoke ball for a specified period. The claimant contracted influenza after having purchased and used one as directed and claimed the reward. The defendants argued, inter alia, that it was impossible to contract with the whole world. This argument was rejected by the court and it was held that the advertisement constituted an offer to the world at large, accepted by the claimant, who was entitled to the £100.

The above decision was relied upon by the Court of Appeal in *Bowerman v Association of British Travel Agents Ltd*, CA, 1995. It was held that the association had made a unilateral offer to prospective customers to provide protection in the event of the financial failure of one of its members. The offer was accepted by booking a holiday with an association member.

A genuine offer must be distinguished from an "invitation to treat"; i.e. where a party is merely inviting offers, which he is then free to accept or reject. The distinction has arisen in the following areas.

Advertisements

Advertisements of goods for sale are normally construed as invitations to treat. In *Partridge v Crittenden* (1968), an advertisement in a periodical which said "Bramblefinches, 25 shillings each" was held to be an invitation to treat and the appellant, who placed the advertisement, was not guilty of the statutory offence of "offering for sale" a wild bird. However, advertisements may be construed as offers if they are of the unilateral type, such as offers for rewards; see the *Carlill* case above.

Circulars, catalogues and price-lists distributed by traders will normally be regarded as invitations to treat; *Grainger and Sons v Gough*, HL, 1896.

Invitations to tender

The courts have held that an invitation to tender will not normally amount to an offer to contract with the party submitting the most favourable tender; *Spencer v Harding* (1870). However, it is now clear that an invitation to tender may amount to an offer of the unilateral type if that is what was clearly intended. In *Harvela Investments Ltd v Royal Trust Co of Canada (CI) Ltd*, HL, 1985, the first defendants invited the claimants and the second defendants to make sealed competitive bids for a parcel of shares, stating, "we bind ourselves to accept (the highest) offer". The claimants bid $2,175,000 and the second defendants bid $2,100,000 or $101,000 "in excess of any other offer". The first defendants believed that they were bound to accept the bid of the second defendants, as being the higher bid. The House of Lords held that the invitation to tender amounted to an offer to sell to the highest bidder; however, the "referential" bid of the type adopted by the second defendants was not permissible in a transaction of this kind and therefore the first defendants were bound to accept the claimants' bid.

A further case on tenders is *Blackpool & Fylde Aero Club Ltd v Blackpool Borough Council*, CA, 1990. Here the defendants invited tenders for an airport concession, laying down a clear procedure for the submission of bids. Due to an administrative error on the part of the defendants, the claimant's bid which had been properly submitted was not considered. The Court of Appeal held that the defendants were contractually bound to consider the claimant's tender.

Auction sales

In an auction, the auctioneer's request for bids is an invitation to treat and each bid is an offer; *Payne v Cave* (1789). This is given statutory force by s.57(2) of the Sale of Goods Act 1979 which states, "a sale by auction is complete when the auctioneer announces its completion by the fall of the hammer, or in other customary manner. Until such announcement is made, any bidder may retract his bid". Similarly, an advertisement that an auction will be held is not an offer; *Harris v Nickerson* (1873). However, in *Warlow v Harrison* (1859) it was stated, *obiter*, that an advertisement to hold an auction "without reserve" would amount to an offer to sell to the highest bidder, accepted by the submission of the highest bid. This approach was followed by the Court of Appeal in *Barry v Heathcote Ball & Co (Commercial Auctions)*, CA, 2000, where it was held that, in a sale without reserve, there was a collateral contract (see Chapter 6) between the auctioneer and the highest bidder. There was consideration both in the form of detriment to the bidder, since his bid could be accepted, and benefit to the auctioneer, as the bidding was driven up. It follows that if the auctioneer refuses to sell to the highest bidder, they will be in breach of contract.

Display of goods

In *Fisher v Bell* (1960), where the defendant was charged with the offence of offering for sale a flick knife, Lord Parker C.J. stated that "the display of an article with a price on it in a shop window is an invitation to treat". The defendant, who had displayed such a knife in his shop, was acquitted. The same principle has been applied by the Court of Appeal to the display of goods in self-service stores; *Pharmaceutical Society of Great Britain v Boots Cash Chemists (Southern) Ltd*, CA, 1953. The main practical consequences of this are that under the law of contract, shops are not bound to sell goods at the price indicated and a customer cannot demand to buy a particular item on display.

Sales of land

In transactions involving land, it is sometimes more difficult to distinguish an offer from what are merely steps in negotiation.

Thus, in one case, a council, in pursuance of a policy of selling council houses, wrote to a tenant, stating that they "may be prepared to sell the house" to him at a stated price. The tenant submitted a formal application but the transaction was broken off at that point by a change in the council's policy. The House of Lords held that there was no contract; the tenant's application was an offer rather than an acceptance; *Gibson v Manchester C.C.*, HL, 1979.

A statement of the minimum price at which a party may be willing to sell will not amount to an offer. In *Harvey v Facey*, P.C., 1893, the claimants cabled the defendants, "Will you sell us Bumper Hall Pen? Telegraph lowest cash price". The defendants replied, "Lowest cash price for Bumper Hall Pen, £900". The claimants then cabled the defendants, "We agree to buy Bumper Hall Pen for the £900 asked by you". It was held that there was not a contract as the second telegram did not constitute an offer.

ACCEPTANCE

Acceptance may be defined as an unconditional assent, communicated by the offeree to the offeror, to all terms of the offer, made with the intention of accepting. Whether an acceptance has in fact occurred is ascertained from the behaviour of the parties, including any correspondence that has passed between them.

It should be noted here that a contract will not be binding unless the parties have expressed themselves with reasonable certainty. The subject of certainty of terms is dealt with in Chapter 6. In relation to acceptance, the courts have developed the following rules.

Acceptance must be unconditional

The offeree must accept the exact terms proposed by the offeror unconditionally; i.e. without introducing any new terms which the offeror has not had the opportunity to consider. The introduction of new terms is referred to as a "counter-offer" and its effect in law is to bring to an end the original offer. For example, in *Hyde v Wrench* (1840), the defendant offered to sell a farm to the claimant for £1,000. In reply, the claimant offered £950. This was rejected by the defendant. Later, the claimant purported to accept the original offer of £1,000. It was held there was no contract; the counter-offer of £950 had impliedly rejected the original offer which was no longer capable of acceptance.

A counter-offer should be distinguished from a mere request for information as in *Stevenson v McLean* (1880) where, in response to an offer to sell goods at a stated price made by the defendants, the claimants replied inquiring whether delivery could be made over two months. No reply to this inquiry was received but the claimants accepted the offer. It was held that there was a binding contract: the claimant's reply was a request for information and not a counter-offer. The counter-offer analysis has been applied to the so-called "battle of the forms" where one party, A, makes an offer on a document containing his standard terms of business and the other party, B, "accepts" on a document containing his (conflicting) standard terms. At this stage, there is clearly no contract, although the courts have held that if B's communication is acted on by A, e.g. by delivery of goods, a contract may come into being on B's terms on the basis that his counter-offer has been accepted; *British Road Services v Arthur Crutchley Ltd*, CA, 1968. This approach was adopted by the Court of Appeal in *Butler Machine Tool Ltd v Excell-o-Corp*, CA, 1979 and in *Pickfords Ltd v Celestica*, CA, 2003.

In *Society of Lloyds v Twinn*, CA, 2000, the offerees purported to accept in one document but attached a covering letter stating that they would not be in a position to pay the sums due under the agreement. The Court of Appeal held that acceptance was sufficiently unconditional; the covering letter sought an indulgence but it was separate and collateral to the concluded contract rather than a condition of acceptance. The question of whether there has been an unconditional acceptance will depend on the facts of the case and the issue must be judged objectively from the language used and the surrounding circumstances.

Acceptance of tenders

We have seen that an invitation to tender is usually, but not invariably, an invitation to treat. Where this is the case, the tender constitutes an offer, however, the "acceptance" of a tender does not always result in a contract. It seems that there are three possibilities:

(1) If a party invites tenders for the supply of a specific quantity of goods on a specific date, then acceptance of the tender results in a binding contract.

(2) If tenders are invited for the supply of a specific quantity of goods over a period of time, then, again, acceptance will conclude a contract.

(3) If the invitation to tender does not specify the quantity of goods, but requires the supply of goods in such quantity as may be ordered from time to time, or "as and when required," then "acceptance" of the tender does not at that stage conclude a contract. Any tender submitted is a "standing offer" which is only accepted in the legal sense when an order is placed for a quantity of goods and there will result a binding contract confined to that quantity; *Percival Ltd v L.C.C. Asylums Committee* (1918). The standing offer may be revoked at any time although the tenderer will be bound by orders already made; *G.N.R. v Witham* (1873).

Acceptance must be communicated

As a general rule, acceptance will not be effective unless communicated to the offeror by the offeree or by someone with his or her authority. An uncommunicated mental assent will not suffice. In *The Leonidas D*, CA, 1985, Goff L.J. said that it is "axiomatic that acceptance of an offer cannot be inferred from silence save in the most exceptional circumstances". The communication of acceptance must be actually received by the offeror, and, where the means of communication are instantaneous (oral, telephone, telex), the contract will come into being when and where acceptance is received; *Entores v Miles Far East Corp*, CA, 1955. A telex message sent out of office hours would not be regarded as instantaneous and the time and place of the formation of the contract would be determined by the intentions of the parties, sound business practice and, possibly, on a judgment as to where the risk would lie; *Brinkibon v Stahag Stahl mbH*, HL, 1983.

The rule that acceptance must be communicated is subject to certain qualifications:

(1) Unilateral contracts. Here there is no requirement that acceptance should be communicated and the performance of the stipulated act will constitute acceptance. Thus, in the *Carlill* case (see above) it was held that the contract was binding even though the claimant did not notify the defendants of her intention to accept.

(2) Need for communication dispensed with. It is possible, in a potentially bilateral contract, for the offeror, expressly or impliedly, to waive the need for communication of accept-

ance by the offeree, e.g. where goods are dispatched in response to an offer to buy. The acceptance in such a case takes place by conduct. It should, however, be clear that the particular conduct was performed by the offeree with the unequivocal intention of accepting the offer; *Taylor v Allon* (1966) and *Day Morris Associates v Voyce*, CA, 2003. In *Anglia Television v Cayton* (1989) it was said that it is a prerequisite of acceptance by conduct that there should be an unequivocal offer in a form capable of unequivocal acceptance. It is for the parties to agree a contract, not for the court to construe one on their behalf.

The above is subject to the reservation that it is not open to the offeror to impose a contract on the offeree against his wishes by deeming that his silence should amount to acceptance. In *Felthouse v Bindley* (1862), the claimant wrote to his nephew offering to buy a horse and saying, "If I hear no more about him, I consider the horse mine at (a stated price)". The nephew did not reply but instructed an auctioneer to keep the horse out of a sale of the nephew's assets. The auctioneer, by mistake, included the horse in the sale and was sued by the claimant for conversion. It was held that the claimant had no title to sue since the nephew had not accepted his offer.

(3) Acceptance by post. This is dealt with below.

Method of acceptance

If the offeror prescribes a particular method of communicating acceptance and makes it clear that no other method will suffice, then there may be no contract if a different method is used by the offeree; *Eliason v Henshaw* (1819).

If, however, a method is prescribed without it being made clear that no other method will suffice, then it seems that an equally advantageous method would suffice. In *Tinn v Hoffman* (1873), it was said that if the offeree was requested to reply "by return of post" then any method which would arrive no later than return of post would do. More recently, the Court of Appeal adopted the same approach in *Yates Building Co Ltd v Pulleyn Ltd*, CA, 1975. It is always open to the offeror, having prescribed a method of acceptance, to waive his right to insist on that method. Such waiver may be express or implied. In some cases the method of acceptance is prescribed by the offeree and inserted for his benefit, as in *Manchester Diocesan*

Council for Education v Commercial and General Investments Ltd (1969). Here the claimants invited tenders, requesting the tenderers to supply an address to which acceptances should be sent. The defendants' tender was accepted but the acceptance was sent to an address different to the one given by the tenderers. This was held to be a good acceptance; the claimants had introduced the prescribed method for their own protection and it could be waived by the claimants providing the defendants were not prejudiced.

Where the offer does not prescribe a method of acceptance, the appropriate method may be inferred from the form in which the offer is made; thus it was said in 1883 that if an offer is sent by telegram, a reply by post would be ineffective; *Quenerduaine v Cole* (1883).

Acceptance by post

A further exception to the rule that acceptance must be communicated is where acceptance is effected by post. The rule is that where acceptance by post has been requested, or where it is an appropriate and reasonable means of communication between the parties, then acceptance is complete immediately the letter of acceptance is posted, even if the letter is delayed, destroyed or lost in the post so that it never reaches the offeror; *Adams v Lindsell* (1818); *Household Fire Insurance (etc.) Co v Grant* (1879). It seems that the rule applies to communications of acceptance by cable, including inland telemessages, but not to instantaneous modes such as telephone, telex, or fax machines.

The "postal rule" is essentially a rule of convenience and is usually justified on the grounds that if the offeror chooses the post as a means of effecting a contract, they must accept the inherent risks. The postal rule will not apply in the situations given below where the court may conclude that the contract comes into being when the letter of acceptance arrives. Where the offer has lapsed by the time the letter of acceptance arrives, then if the postal rule does not apply, there may be no contract at all.

The postal rule will not apply:

(1) where the letter of acceptance has not been properly posted, as in *Re London and Northern Bank* (1900), where the letter of acceptance was handed to a postman only authorised to deliver;

(2) where the letter is not properly addressed. There is no direct authority on this point but the analogous case of *Getreideimport Gmbh v Contimar* (1953) would support this view. G. H. Treitel has suggested that an inflexible rule on this point might in some cases prejudice the offeror and the better rule is that a misdirected acceptance should take effect, if at all, at the time least favourable to the party responsible for misdirection;

(3) where the express terms of the offer exclude the postal rule, i.e. if the offer specifies that the acceptance must reach the offeror. In *Holwell Securities v Hughes*, CA, 1974, the postal rule was held not to apply where the offer was to be accepted by "notice in writing". Actual communication was required;

(4) where it is unreasonable to use the post; e.g. to reply by second class post to a verbal or cabled offer, or to accept by post on the eve of a postal strike. Further, it was said in *Holwell's* case (above) that the rule would not be applied where it would produce a "manifest inconvenience or absurdity".

Although there is no English authority on the point, it does not seem possible, where the postal rule applies, for the offeree, having posted his acceptance, then to revoke it by some quicker means of communication, such as by telephone. The Scottish case of *Dunmore v Alexander* (1830), which appears to permit such a revocation, is unreliable as the majority of the court appear to have decided the case on the basis that there had been the revocation of an offer.

Email

Communications by email bear some resemblance to postal communications in that the message is sent via an on-line server (akin to an electronic sorting office) and may not be immediately received. If the postal rule applied, the contract would come into being at the moment the offeree's mouse clicked on the "send" button. However, since the sender will generally know if his message has not been sent, it seems preferable to apply the rule relating to instantaneous modes (see above), i.e. that the contract will not come into being until the acceptance has been received. This raises the issue of precisely when the message can be said to have been received; is it when the message is transmitted to the server; to the offeror's computer; or when it is actually read? Given the practical problems that may arise, the second of these three possibilities would appear to be the most sensible.

Acceptance must be given in exchange for the offer

Where there is an offer of the unilateral type, the question arises as to whether there is a contract where a person fulfils the condition contained in the offer without knowledge that the offer has been made.

In the American case of *Fitch v Snedaker* (1868) it was ruled that a person who gives information without knowledge of the offer of a reward cannot claim the reward. In the Australian case, *R. v Clarke* (1927), the principle was extended to the case of a person who had once known of the offer but at the time of the purported acceptance it had "passed from his mind". Despite the apparently contrary decision in *Gibbons v Proctor* (1891), English law is thought to be in accordance with *Fitch's* case. Motive, however, is not relevant; in *Williams v Carwardine* (1833) it was held that the claimant was entitled to a reward even though she gave the information out of a motive of spite. A similar problem is that of identical cross-offers, i.e. where A offers to sell and Y offers to buy the same goods on the same terms, each offer being made in ignorance of the other, the offers crossing in the post. It is thought that no contract would be formed on these facts as there is no true offer and acceptance; *Tinn v Hoffmann* (1873).

TERMINATION OF OFFER

Unless accepted, an offer has no legal effect. Apart from counter-offer (already discussed) and express rejection, an offer may terminate in the following ways.

Revocation

An offer may be revoked at any time until it is accepted. In *Routledge v Grant* (1828) it was held that a promise to keep the offer open for a period of time will not be binding unless supported by consideration. Further, revocation will only be effective if communicated to the offeree. Thus, in *Byrne v Van Tienhoven* (1880), the defendants made an offer to the claimants by letter on October 1. The claimants received the letter on

October 11, and immediately accepted by telegram. Meanwhile on October 8, the defendants had sent a letter revoking their offer, which arrived on October 20. It was held there was a binding contract since revocation was ineffective until communicated but acceptance was effective as from October 11.

Communication of revocation need not be made by the offeror personally; it may be sufficient if revocation is communicated by some reliable third party; *Dickinson v Dodds*, CA, 1876. Where the offer is made to the public at large, as in a unilateral contract, it may be validly revoked by taking reasonable steps to notify persons who might be likely to accept; *Shuey v U.S.* (1875).

In unilateral contracts, where acceptance is denoted by the performance of some stipulated act, the question arises as to when acceptance is effective so as to prevent the offeror from revoking, i.e. at the commencement or on completion of the act. Various solutions have been advanced but the general rule would seem to be, as a result of *Offord v Davis* (1862) and *Errington v Errington*, CA, 1952 that, once the offeree has commenced performance, the offeror may not revoke. In Errington, a father financed the purchase of a house by mortgage, and allowed his daughter and son-in-law to live in it, on terms that if they paid off all the mortgage repayments, the house would be theirs. The couple made no counter-promise and so the contract was unilateral. The Court of Appeal held that once the couple commenced and continued making the repayments, the offer could not be revoked. However, the father would not be liable on his promise until performance of the stipulated act was complete; i.e. in the above case, when all the repayments were made. In *Daulia Ltd v Four Millbank Nominees Ltd*, CA, 1978, the Court of Appeal, *obiter*, accepted the above analysis. The rule stated above is a general one and would not be applied where it was contrary to the parties' intentions, e.g. estate agency commission agreements; *Luxor (Eastbourne) Ltd v Cooper*, HL, 1941.

Lapse

An offer will lapse either after a fixed period for which it has been left open, or, in the absence of a fixed period, after a reasonable length of time has passed. What is reasonable will depend upon the circumstances of the offer and the subject-matter; thus an offer to buy perishable goods or a commodity where the price fluctuates daily will lapse fairly quickly. In *Ramsgate Victoria Hotel v Montefiori* (1866), an offer to buy shares could not be accepted after the expiry of five months from when it was made; the offer was held to have lapsed.

An offer may also lapse if it is made subject to a condition which then fails. In *Financings Ltd v Stimson*, CA, 1962 an offer to sell a car on hire-purchase was held to be subject to an implied condition that the car remained undamaged until the moment of acceptance. As this condition had been broken there was no contract.

Death

If the offeror dies before acceptance, there is authority that the offeree may validly accept providing; (i) it is not a contract involving the personal service of the offeror; and (ii) the offeree has not been notified of the death; *Bradbury v Morgan* (1862).

There is, however, a dictum to the contrary in *Dickinson v Dodds* (1876), per Mellish L.J., ". . . if a man who makes an offer dies, the offer cannot be accepted after he is dead".

If the offeree dies before acceptance, then it seems the offer will terminate and cannot be accepted by his personal representatives.

ANOMALOUS CASES

In *Gibson v Manchester C.C.*, HL, 1979, the House of Lords recognised that there may be certain exceptional types of case where, although it is clear that the parties have reached agreement, it is difficult to discern an offer and acceptance. An example is *Clarke v Dunraven*, HL, 1897, where the rules of a yacht club were held to form the basis of a binding contract between each member, one to another, and in *Brogden v Metropolitan Railway*, HL, 1877, the House of Lords inferred a contract from the conduct of the parties although there had been no actual acceptance. The possibility of a contract coming into being during and as a result of performance was confirmed in *G. Percy Trentham Ltd v Archital Luxfer*, CA, 1993.

3. INTENTION TO BE LEGALLY BOUND

The courts have recognised that some agreements, by their very nature, are not intended to be legally binding and in others the parties may expressly declare or indicate that they do not intend to assume contractual relations.

The case law in this area establishes that, despite doubts expressed by some academic writers, the intention to contract is a necessary independent element in the formation of a contract. The cases may be classified under five heads.

ADVERTISEMENTS

For the purpose of attracting custom, tradesmen may make vague exaggerated claims in advertisements. Such statements are essentially statements of opinion or "mere puff" and are not intended to form the basis of a binding contract. It should be noted, however, that even a precise statement will not be binding if it is clear that it was not seriously meant; in *Weeks v Tybald* (1605) the defendant was not bound when he offered £100 to the man who would marry his daughter with his consent.

Even in advertisements, the court will look for evidence of contractual intent, thus in *Carlill's* case (see Chapter 2), the company's defence that their advertisement was mere puff was rejected by the court on the ground that the company had deposited £1,000 in a bank as proof of their sincerity.

DOMESTIC AGREEMENTS

Agreements between a husband and wife living together as one household are presumed not to be intended to be legally binding, unless the agreement states to the contrary. In *Balfour v Balfour*, CA, 1919, a husband who was posted abroad, leaving his wife to stay in England due to ill-health, was held not bound to pay her a promised monthly allowance. The presumption against contractual intention, as in *Merritt v Merritt*, CA, 1969, will not apply where the spouses are not living together in amity at the time of the agreement.

It seems that agreements of a domestic nature between parent and child are likewise presumed not to be intended to be binding; *Jones v Padavatton*, CA, 1969. Where the parties to the agreement share a household but are not related, the court will examine all the circumstances; in *Simpkins v Pays* (1955), an agreement between the members of a household to share the winnings of a competition they jointly entered was held to be legally binding.

Where members of a family have a business relationship with each other there will be contractual intention in relation to contracts of a business, as opposed to a domestic, nature; *Snelling v John G. Snelling Ltd* (1972).

SOCIAL AGREEMENTS

It is recognised that there is a sphere of social arrangements where contractual relations are not intended; "To offer a friend a meal is not to invite litigation". (Cheshire and Fifoot.) This presumption against contractual intention has been applied by the courts to a variety of arrangements including a golf competition (*Lens v The Devonshire Club* (1914)) and to an arrangement for sharing petrol costs where a person is given a lift to work; *Coward v Motor Insurers' Bureau*, CA, 1963. In neither case was there held to be a contract.

COMMERCIAL AGREEMENTS

In commercial agreements, there is a strong presumption that the parties intend to be legally bound. This presumption may generally only be rebutted by express words, as in *Rose and Frank Co v Crompton Bros. Ltd*, HL, 1925, where the parties provided that a sole-agency agreement should "not be subject to legal jurisdiction in the law courts". The House of Lords considered that the clear words used rebutted the presumption. Similarly, football pools stated to be "binding in honour only" are not legal contracts so that a participant may not recover the winnings; *Jones v Vernon's Pools* (1938).

The onus of rebutting contractual intent is a heavy one; in *Edwards v Skyways Ltd* (1964), a redundancy agreement providing for an ex gratia payment to be made to an employee was held to be a binding contract; the expression used was insufficient to rebut contractual intention. *Esso Petroleum Ltd v Commissioners of Customs and Excise*, HL, 1976 shows the difficulty of rebutting contractual intention where clear words are not used. Esso distributed World Cup coins to be given free to any motorist who purchased a given amount of petrol. The House of Lords was divided on the issue of contractual intention.

In *Kleinwort Benson Ltd v Malaysia Mining Corp*, CA, 1989 it was held that a "letter of comfort", where a company stated that it was its policy to ensure that its subsidiary could meet its liability in respect of loans made to it, did not have contractual effect. The words in question were intended as a statement of existing fact and not as a contractual promise.

The issue of intention arose in *Edmonds v Lawson*, CA, 2000. A pupil barrister contended that pupillage constituted a "contract of employment" under s.54(3)(a) of the National Minimum Wage Act 1998. Even though pupils are generally unpaid, the Court of Appeal held that there was an intention to create legal relations. Pupils provided consideration for the offer made by chambers by agreeing to enter the productive relationship which pupillage involved. However, pupillage was not a contract of apprenticeship and the claimant was not a "worker" within the meaning of the 1998 Act. There was therefore no entitlement to receive the national minimum wage.

COLLECTIVE AGREEMENTS

A collective agreement is an agreement between a trade union and an employer regulating rates of pay and conditions of work. If the terms of such an agreement are incorporated into an individual employee's contract of service, they will be legally binding on the parties. With regard to the agreement itself, the position at common law was that collective agreements were not intended to be legally binding between union and employer; *Ford Motor Co Ltd v A.U.E.F.W.* (1969).

The position at common law has been affirmed by statute: under s.179(1) and (2) of the Trade Union and Labour Relations (Consolidation) Act 1992, a collective agreement is presumed not to have been intended by the parties to be a legally enforceable contract unless it is in writing and expressly provides to the contrary.

4. CONSIDERATION

In addition to offer and acceptance and contractual intent, consideration is an essential element in the formation of any contract not by deed.

English law will not enforce a gratuitous or "bare" promise. By way of example, if one party, A (the promisor), promises to mow the lawn of another, B (the promisee), A's promise will only be enforceable by B as a contract if B has provided consideration. The consideration from B might normally take the form of a payment of money but could consist of some other service to which A might agree. Further, the promise of a money payment or service in the future is just as sufficient a consideration as payment itself or the actual rendering of the service. Thus, the promisee has to give something in return for the promise of the promisor in order to convert a bare promise made in his favour into a binding contract.

It follows that English law requires a simple contract to be a bargain and this aspect is stressed in the definition of Pollock, approved by *Lord Dunedin in Dunlop v Selfridge Ltd*, HL, 1915: "an act or forbearance of one party, or the promise thereof, is the price for which the promise of the other is bought, and the promise thus given for value is enforceable".

Another definition (given by Lush J. in *Currie v Misa* (1875)) refers to consideration as consisting of a detriment to the promisee or a benefit to the promisor: ". . . some right, interest, profit or benefit accruing to the one party, or some forbearance, detriment, loss or responsibility given, suffered or undertaken by the other". It should be noted that the words "benefit" and "detriment" do not refer to whether or not the bargain is an advantageous one; thus a person who, in return for a money payment, promises to abstain from smoking will legally incur a detriment and provide consideration even though the promise is beneficial to his health. If he has never smoked anyway, then it is doubtful whether he could be said to incur a detriment; see *Arrale v Costain Civil Engineering Ltd* (1975).

The definition of Lush J. referred to above speaks of benefit and detriment as alternatives; it might be more accurate to say that whilst consideration may consist of a benefit to the promisor, it must always consist of a detriment to the promisee because of the rule (discussed below) that consideration must always move from the promisee.

TYPES OF CONSIDERATION

Consideration is called "executory" where there is an exchange of promises to perform acts in the future, e.g. a bilateral contract for the supply of goods whereby A promises to deliver goods to B at a future date and B promises to pay on delivery. Alternatively, consideration is referred to as "executed" where one party performs an act in fulfilment of a promise made by the other, e.g. the unilateral contract where A offers a reward to anyone who provides certain information. Both these types of consideration should be distinguished from "past" consideration which is discussed below.

JUDICIAL RULES RELATING TO CONSIDERATION

The courts have developed certain technical rules in relation to consideration:

Consideration must not be past

Past consideration, unlike executory or executed consideration, is not good or valid consideration. Consideration is said to be past when it consists of some service or benefit previously rendered to the promisor. Whether consideration is past is a question of fact. In *Re McArdle*, CA, 1951, a woman carried out work to a house jointly owned by members of her family. After the work had been completed, her relatives signed a document promising to pay her for the work. It was held that she could not recover the sum promised as her consideration was past.

If, however, the service is performed at the defendant's request and in circumstances where both parties understand that payment will follow, the court may be prepared to enforce the transaction: *Lampleigh v Braithwait* (1615); *Kennedy v Broun* (1863). Thus, if, in *Re McArdle*, the woman had been first requested by her relatives to carry out the work, the consideration may not have been regarded as past. The law on this point is substantially contained in Re Casey's Patents, *Stewart v Casey*, CA, 1892. Patent owners wrote to their manager, "in consideration of your (past) services . . . as manager", they would give him a one-third share. The Court of Appeal rejected the patent owners' submission that the services were past consideration. The original request being implied, the performance of the services had raised an implication that they would be paid for and the subsequent express promise to pay merely fixed the amount. This decision was affirmed by the *Privy Council in Pau On v Lau Yiu Long*, PC, 1980.

Two statutory exceptions to the rule about past consideration should be noted:

(1) Section 27 of the Bills of Exchange Act 1882 provides that an antecedent debt or liability will support a bill of exchange; and

(2) Section 29 and 30 of the Limitation Act 1980 provide that where a debt is acknowledged within the statutory limitation period (see Chapter 14) the limitation period begins to run again from the date of acknowledgment.

Consideration must move from the promisee

Only a person who has provided consideration in return for a promise may enforce that promise as a contract. In *Tweddle v Atkinson* (1861), Guy agreed with John Tweddle that they would each pay a sum to Tweddle's son William, who was Guy's prospective son-in-law. William's action against Guy's executors failed as no consideration had moved from him.

It may well be thought that the principle in the above case is in effect the same principle as the rule of "privity of contract", however the courts have treated them as distinct. It should be noted that under the provisions of the Contracts (Rights of Third Parties) Act 1999, a third party who can bring him or herself within the terms of the legislation may well have an enforceable action in cases such as *Tweddle v Atkinson* (see Chapter 12).

Consideration need not be adequate

Providing consideration has some value, the courts will not investigate its adequacy. A contract is a bargain freely entered into and the courts are not concerned with whether it constitutes a good bargain. Where consideration is recognised by the law as having some value it is described as "real" or "sufficient" consideration. For example, a rent of £1 per annum (a "peppercorn" rent) would be sufficient consideration for the grant of lease on premises worth thousands, providing, of course, the transaction was entered into freely. In *Chappell & Co Ltd v Nestle Co Ltd*, HL, 1960, the House of Lords considered, in a copyright case, that used chocolate wrappers were part of the consideration for the purchase of a gramophone record. Similar examples of relatively trivial but sufficient consideration include the promise to surrender a document believed to be valuable but in fact of no legal effect (*Haigh v Brooks* (1839)); the temporary and apparently purposeless deprivation of a chattel (*Bainbridge v Firmstone* (1838)) and the possibility that the publication of a letter in a newspaper might increase the paper's circulation; *De La Bere v Pearson Ltd*, CA, 1908.

It is well-established that if, in civil proceedings, a person with a valid claim against another (e.g. in contract or tort), promises to forbear from enforcing it, this will constitute consideration for a promise to settle the claim made by the other. The position may well be the same where there is no actual promise to forbear but the person with the claim actually forbears, providing the forbearance is clearly given in exchange for the promise of the other party, *Alliance Bank Ltd v Broom* (1864). The courts have also held that a promise not to pursue an invalid claim (i.e. one that would fail at law) may constitute sufficient consideration for a promise to settle by the other party; *Callisher v Bischoffsheim* (1870). There are, however, certain provisos, in particular that the potential claimant has a bona fide belief in the prospect of the claim succeeding (*Horton v Horton*, CA, 1961) and that he has made full and honest disclosure to the potential defendant of matters which might affect the validity of the claim; *Miles v N.Z. Alford Estate Co* (1886).

We have seen that, in order to be sufficient, consideration must have some value, however trivial. However, if the consideration is empty or illusory, or concerned with human feelings, the courts have tended to regard it as insufficient. It is sometimes said that consideration must have some "economic" value, though this formulation is perhaps a little narrow. In *White v Bluett* (1853), a son's promise not to bore his father with complaints was held not to be sufficient consideration for a promise by the father to discharge the son's debts; in *Thomas v Thomas* (1842), a husband's desire that his widow should live in his house after his death was held not to be part of the consideration for the executor's promise that she could do so. *Eastwood v Kenyon* (1840) is a similar decision where the court refused to recognise a moral obligation as a sufficient consideration to enforce a promise to pay a sum of money.

Another group of cases where consideration has been held to be insufficient is where it consists of a promise to perform, or the performance of, some existing duty already owed by the promisee to the promisor, either as a result of some public duty or under an existing contract with the promisor. These cases will be dealt with below.

Existing public duty

Collins v Godefroy (1831) is usually cited as authority for the proposition that the performance of an existing public duty is not consideration. In that case, the defendant promised to pay the claimant a sum of money for giving evidence in a court action in which the claimant had been subpoenaed. As the claimant was under a legal duty to attend court, it was held that he had not furnished consideration. There are, however, suggestions in other cases (e.g. *Morgan v Palmer* (1824)) that the real reason for the law refusing to enforce such contracts is that they are contrary to public policy.

Consideration will be furnished when an existing public duty is exceeded. Thus, if the police agree to provide a colliery with extra protection during a miners' strike, they provide consideration for a promise to pay them for that extra service; *Glasbrook Bros v Glamorgan C.C.*, HL, 1925. In *Ward v Byham*, CA, 1956, the mother of an illegitimate child promised the father, in return for a weekly allowance, that she would keep the child "well-looked-after and happy". It was held, by the majority of the Court of Appeal, that the mother had provided consideration in that she had promised to exceed her statutory duty, which was merely to "maintain" the child (cf. *White v Bluett* (above)). Lord Denning, in this case, thought the agreement enforceable, but on the unorthodox ground that a promise to perform an existing duty is good consideration as it is a benefit to the person to whom it is given.

Existing contractual duty

The rule here is that the performance of an existing contractual duty owed to the promisor is not sufficient consideration. Authority for the principle is to be found in *Stilk v Myrick* (1809), where two sailors deserted a ship and the captain promised the remaining eight crew members extra wages if they would work the ship home. They were already bound to do this under their contracts and it was held that the captain's promise was not binding. The reports of the case reveal two bases for the decision, (i) that the crew had given no consideration, as they were already bound to work the ship home; and (ii) that the promise could not be enforced as it was contrary to public policy. The lack of consideration theory receives modern support from *Swain v West (Butchers) Ltd* (1936) and *North Ocean Shipping Co Ltd v Hyundai Construction Co Ltd* (1979) although that decision was based on economic duress (see Chapter 10).

In *Hartley v Ponsonby* (1857) it was held, in another "seamen's wages" case, that there was consideration for the promise to pay extra wages. The desertion of half the crew had rendered the ship short-handed and so the voyage became more dangerous. Existing contractual duty had been exceeded and effectively a fresh bargain had been entered into.

In *Williams v Roffey and Nicholls (Contractors) Ltd*, CA, 1990, a "qualification" to *Stilk v Myrick* was introduced whereby if the performance of an existing contractual duty confers a practical benefit on the other party this can constitute valid consideration. The defendants were building contractors refurbishing 27 flats. They contracted with the claimant to carry out joinery work for £20,000. The defendants' main contract contained a time penalty clause and they were concerned that the claimant would not complete the work on time. Consequently, the defendants promised to pay the claimant a £10,300 bonus if he completed on time. The claimant carried out the work but the defendants did not pay the bonus. It was held by the Court of Appeal that the claimant had provided consideration by completing the work on time. Glidewell L.J. held that:

(1) if A has entered into a contract with B to do work for, or supply goods and services to, B in return for payment by B; and

(2) at some stage before A has completely performed his obligations under the contract, B has reason to doubt whether A will, or will be able to, complete his side of the bargain; and

(3) B thereupon promises A an additional payment in return for A's promise to perform his contractual obligations on time; and

(4) as a result of giving his promise, B obtains in practice a benefit, or obviates a disbenefit; and

(5) B's promise is not given as a result of economic duress or fraud on the part of A; then

(6) the benefit to B is capable of being consideration for B's promise, so that the promise will be legally binding.

Existing contractual duty owed to a third party

There is clear authority that the performance, or the promise to perform, an existing contractual duty owed by the promisee to a third party, is good consideration.

In *Scotson v Pegg* (1861), A agreed to deliver coal to B, or to B's order. B ordered A to deliver the coal to C. C promised A that if A would deliver the coal, he would unload it. In an action by A to enforce C's promise, it was held that A's delivery of the coal (the performance of an existing contractual duty to a third party, B) was good consideration to enforce C's promise. Further, but more dubious, support for the existence of the rule is to be found in *Shadwell v Shadwell* (1860), and two modern Privy Council decisions expressly approve *Scotson v Pegg*. These are *New Zealand Shipping Co Ltd v A.M. Satterthwaite Co Ltd*, PC, 1975 and *Pau On v Lau Yiu Long*, PC, 1980, as a result of which it would seem that the principle is firmly established.

PART-PAYMENT OF DEBTS

The discharge of debts gives rise to certain problems concerning consideration.

The rule at common law (the rule in *Pinnel's* case (1602)) is that the part-payment of a debt is not good consideration for a promise to forgo the balance. Thus, if A owes B £50 and B accepts £25 in full satisfaction on the due date, there is nothing to prevent B from claiming the balance at a later date, since there is no consideration proceeding from A to enforce the promise of B to accept part payment. However, it was held in *Pinnel's* case that the agreement to accept part-payment would be binding if A, at B's request, provided some fresh consideration. Consideration might be provided if:

(1) B agrees to accept part-payment on an earlier date than the due date (i.e. as in *Pinnel's* case itself); or
(2) B agrees to accept a chattel instead of money (even if worth less than the debt since consideration need not be adequate); or
(3) B agrees to accept part-payment in a different place to that originally specified.

Until 1966 it used to be the rule that part-payment by cheque, as opposed to notes and coins, was sufficient consideration to discharge a debt. As a result of *D. and C.*

Builders v Rees, CA, 1966, overruling earlier cases, the position is now that part payment by cheque does not, without more, discharge a debt.

Despite its harshness and lack of commercial reality, the rule in *Pinnel's* case was affirmed by the House of Lords in *Foakes v Beer*, HL, 1884 and still represents the law. It is, however, subject to a possible exception in equity, to be discussed below ("promissory estoppel"). The rule was considered recently in *Re Selectmove*, CA, 1995 where the court declined to extend the principle in *Williams v Roffey* (see above) to the part-payment of debts. Peter Gibson L.J. considered that such an extension would in effect leave the principle in *Foakes v Beer* without any application.

There are two exceptions at common law to the rule in *Pinnel's* case:

(1) Composition agreements. Here a group of creditors who are owed money by a single debtor agree to accept, say 50p in the pound in absolute discharge. Despite the absence of consideration, it is established that no individual creditor can subsequently sue the debtor for the balance owed to him; *Wood v Robarts* (1818). The reason usually advanced for the rule is essentially a "policy" one, that to allow an individual creditor to claim the balance would amount to a fraud on the other creditors.

(2) Part-payment of the debt by a third party. If accepted by the creditor in full settlement, part-payment by a third party affords a defence in an action by the creditor to recover the balance. In *Welby v Drake* (1825), the defendant was indebted to the claimant. The claimant agreed with the defendant's father to accept part-payment by the father in full satisfaction of his son's debt. The money having been paid, it was held that the claimant could not recover the balance from the defendant, as by suing the defendant son, he would commit a fraud on the father.

PROMISSORY ESTOPPEL

A further, and controversial, exception to the rule in *Pinnel's* case is to be found in the equitable doctrine of promissory estoppel. The doctrine provides a means of making a promise binding, in certain circumstances, in the absence of consideration.

The modern doctrine is largely based on dicta of Denning J. in *Central London Property Trust Ltd v High Trees House Ltd* (1947) and on the decision of the House of Lords in *Tool Metal Manufacturing Co Ltd v Tungsten Electric Co Ltd*, HL, 1955 and can be traced to *Hughes v Metropolitan Railway*, HL, 1877.

In *Hughes v Metropolitan Railway*, a landlord gave his tenant six months' notice to repair and in the event of a failure to repair, the lease would be forfeited. Within the six months, the landlord opened negotiations with the tenant for the sale of the lease, during which time the tenant carried out no repairs. Shortly after, negotiations broke down and at the end of the six-months' notice period, the landlord claimed to forfeit the lease.

The House of Lords held that the landlord could not do so. The landlord had, by his conduct, led the tenant to suppose that the landlord would not enforce forfeiture at the end of the notice period and the tenant had relied on this by not carrying out repairs. However, the six-month period would begin to run again from the date of the breakdown of negotiations.

The doctrine in *Hughes* is, in effect, a form of equitable or "promissory" estoppel with less strict requirements than common law estoppel which could only arise from a representation of existing fact and not from a promise as to future conduct or intention; *Jorden v Money*, HL, 1854. The doctrine operates where there has been a representation by one party (the promisor) that they do not intend to enforce their strict legal rights, made with the intention that the other party (the promisee) will rely on the representation, and the other party does in fact rely upon the representation without providing consideration. The party making the representation will be estopped from enforcing his or her strict legal rights, in so far as it is inequitable to do so.

Hughes v Metropolitan Railway was relied on in the *High Trees* case. Here landlords of a block of flats agreed to accept from the tenants half the ground rent stipulated in the lease because of wartime conditions (shortage of sub-tenants). It was held by Denning J. that by the end of the war the landlords were entitled to the full rent as the circumstances which gave rise to the rent reduction were no longer in existence. Despite the absence of consideration, the judge said, *obiter*, that if the landlords had sought to recover the balance of rent falling due during the war years, when only half the rent had been paid, they would have been estopped in equity. *High Trees* takes the Hughes doctrine perhaps a stage further as it envisages the extinguishment of the right to receive sums contractually due, i.e. the balance of ground rent.

The exact scope of the doctrine of promissory estoppel is a matter of debate but it is clear that certain requirements must be satisfied before the doctrine can come into play:

(1) There must be a clear and unambiguous statement by the promisor that his or her strict legal rights will not be enforced; *Scandinavian Trading Tanker Co A.B. v Flota Petrolera Ecuatoriana*, HL, 1983.

(2) The promisee must have acted in reliance on the promise. There is some uncertainty as to whether the promisee should have relied on the promise by changing position to their detriment (i.e. so that they are put in a worse position if the promise is revoked) or whether they should merely have altered their position in some way, not necessarily for the worse. In *W. J. Alan Co Ltd v El Nasr Export and Import Co*, CA, 1972, Lord Denning M.R. said that "he must have been led to act differently from what he otherwise would have done". However, in the absence of detriment, it might be difficult to show that it is inequitable for the promisor to go back on his or her word; see (3), below.

(3) It must be inequitable for the promisor to go back on his or her word and revert to his or her strict legal rights. In *D. and C. Builders v Rees*, CA, 1966, the debtor took advantage of the creditors' financial straits to pressure them into accepting part-payment. In an action for the balance of the money owed, Lord Denning M.R. was of the view that it was not inequitable for the creditors to go back on their word and claim the balance as the debtor had acted inequitably by exerting improper pressure.

(4) The doctrine may only be raised as a defence; "as a shield and not a sword". It was held in *Combe v Combe*, CA, 1951 that the doctrine cannot be raised as a cause of action and therefore it does not dispense with the requirement of consideration in the formation of contracts. This decision was affirmed by the Court of Appeal in *Baird Textile Holdings v Marks and Spencer Plc*, CA, 2001.

It has never been conclusively determined whether the doctrine may be applied to extinguish permanently the right to the balance of a lump sum debt after part-payment, or whether it merely suspends the creditor's rights until such time as it is equitable to claim the balance. Where the debtor's contractual obligation is to make periodic payments, the creditor's right to receive payments during the period of suspension may be permanently extinguished, but the creditor may revert to his or her strict contractual rights either upon giving reasonable notice, or where the circumstances which give rise to the promise have changed (as in *High Trees*). In the *Tool Metal* case, patent owners promised to suspend periodic payments of compensation due to them from manufacturers from the outbreak of war. It was held that the promise was binding during the period of suspension, but the owners could, on giving reasonable notice to the other party, revert to their legal entitlement to receive the compensation payments.

It had always been assumed that promissory estoppel could only arise where there was some contractual or pre-existing legal relationship between the parties. In *Brikom Investments Ltd v Carr*, CA, 1979, Lord Denning M.R. was of the view that the doctrine can apply to promises made by parties negotiating for a contract, i.e. who are not yet in any legal relationship with each other. Such an extension of the doctrine is difficult to reconcile with the law relating to pre-contractual representations (see Chapter 6).

5. CAPACITY AND FORMALITIES

CAPACITY

The law requires persons entering a contract to have the necessary capacity. All persons of full age have contractual capacity. There are three special cases: corporations; persons of unsound mind including drunkards; and minors.

Corporations

Corporations are classified, according to the manner in which they are created, into registered, statutory and chartered.

1. Registered companies. Companies registered under the Companies Act 1985 have capacity to enter into any contract that is within the limits of the "objects" clause of the company's memorandum of association. This is a public document without which a company cannot be registered.

At common law, a company that contracted outside these limits acted ultra vires and any transaction entered into was void; *Ashbury Railway Carriage and Iron Co v Riche*, HL, 1925. However, the Companies Act 1985, s.35 (as amended by the Companies Act 1989), now provides that an ultra vires contract may be enforceable against a company by a person dealing with the company in good faith, providing the transaction has been decided upon by the directors.

2. Statutory corporations. These are corporations created by Act of Parliament. The contractual capacity of such corporations is to be found in the incorporating statute; any contract entered into outside the powers contained in the statute is ultra vires and void.

3. Chartered corporations. Corporations set up by Royal Charter (e.g. charitable associations and some universities) possess the same contractual capacity as a natural person of full age and capacity.

Persons of unsound mind and drunkards

As a general rule, a contract with a person suffering from mental disability or drunkenness is valid, unless the person is, at the time of the contract, incapable of understanding the nature of the transaction and the other party is aware of this; *Molton v Camroux* (1849). In such circumstances, the contract is voidable at the insane or drunken person's option.

Where, however, the other (sane) party is unaware of the other's disability, the contract will be judged by the same standards as if the contract were between two persons of sound minds; *Hart v O'Connor*, PC, 1985. Thus, the transaction would only be set aside if unconscionable (see Chapter 10).

Section 3 of the Sale of Goods Act 1979 provides that persons under such disability will be liable to pay a reasonable sum for necessary goods sold and delivered to them.

Minors

Persons below the age of 18 are regarded in law as minors (or infants). With the lowering, in 1969, of the age of majority to 18, this topic has ceased to have the same practical significance as formerly.

Contracts made with minors fall into three categories; those that are: Contracts valid at common law; Contracts voidable at common law and Other contracts.

1. Contracts valid at common law.   Contracts for the sale of necessary goods sold and actually delivered to the minor are binding upon him or her. Necessary goods are those suitable to the minor's station in life and his or her actual requirements at the time of delivery; *Nash v Inman* (1908). The minor's obligation is to pay a reasonable price for the goods, not necessarily the contract price.

The minor is likewise bound to pay a reasonable sum for necessary services, although in this case the contract is binding even if only executory; *Roberts v Gray*, CA, 1913.

The minor is also bound by beneficial contracts of service, apprenticeship and analogous contracts.

2. Contracts voidable at common law.   Certain contracts are voidable at the instance of the minor. These are contracts for the sale or purchase of land; leases; contracts to buy shares; marriage settlements and partnership agreements.

Such contracts are enforceable by the minor, and binding upon him or her unless repudiated during minority or within a reasonable time after attaining majority.

3. Other contracts. At common law other contracts were also said to be "voidable" but in the sense that they were not binding on the minor unless ratified by him or her on attaining majority. However, the Infants Relief Act 1874 rendered loans and contracts for the supply of non-necessary goods entered into by minors "absolutely void". This Act was not without its difficulties and was repealed by the Minors Contracts Act 1987, s.1 and therefore the common law position referred to above once again applies. The position at common law with regard to the contracts referred to in 1. and 2. (above) also remains unchanged.

Section 2 of the 1987 Act overrules *Coutts v Browne-Lecky* (1947) and renders guarantees made by adults of loans advanced to minors enforceable against the adult guarantor. Section 3 provides a restitutionary remedy for an adult who has entered into an enforceable contract with a minor. Before the Act non-necessary goods acquired by the minor were generally irrecoverable by the adult party even where the minor had lied about his or her age: *Leslie v Shiell*, CA, 1914. However, the court may now, if just and equitable, require the minor to transfer to the adult any property acquired by the minor under the contract or any property representing it.

FORMALITIES

As a general rule, the law does not require any formalities (i.e. writing) to render a contract valid and enforceable. Nevertheless, certain contracts are required to be by deed, others to be in writing and one type of contract is required to be evidenced in writing.

Contracts which must be by deed

A lease for more than three years must be made by deed, and if not by deed, is void for the purpose of creating a legal estate. Gratuitous promises (i.e. without consideration) may be rendered enforceable by a deed.

Contracts which must be in writing

A contract may be required to be made in a written form by the provisions of a statute. For example, the Consumer Credit Act 1974 requires consumer credit agreements to be made in a certain form. An agreement which is not properly executed in accordance with the Act can only be enforced against the debtor on an order of the court.

Until 1989 contracts for the sale or other disposition of an interest in land were required to be evidenced in writing by virtue of s.40 of the Law of Property Act 1925, although the requirement goes back to the Statute of Frauds 1677. Even where there was insufficient written evidence the contract might nevertheless be enforceable under the equitable doctrine of part-performance. The Law Reform (Miscellaneous Provisions) Act 1989, which came into force on September 27, 1989, repealed s.40 L.P.A. 1925 and sets out new rules governing formalities which will be required for all contracts for the sale or other disposition of an interest in land. The equitable doctrine of part-performance disappeared.

The basic requirement of the regime is that all contracts relating to interests in land must be written and signed by the parties. Section 2 provides:

(1) A contract for the sale or other disposition of an interest in land can only be made in writing and only by incorporating all the terms which the parties have expressly agreed in one document or, where contracts are exchanged, in each.
(2) The terms may be incorporated in a document either by being set out in it or by reference to some other document.
(3) The document incorporating the terms, or, where contracts are exchanged, one of the documents incorporating them (but not necessarily the same one) must be signed by, or on behalf of, each party to the contract.

In *Spiro v Glencrown Properties Ltd* (1991) it was held that the requirements of s.2 applied to the grant of an option for the sale of land.

Excluded from the new rules are:

(1) contracts for the grant of leases of three years or less;
(2) contracts regulated under the Financial Services Act 1986;
(3) contracts made in the course of a public auction.

Contracts which must be evidenced in writing

Contracts of guarantee are required by statute to be "evidenced in writing". The requirement of written evidence means that there must be some written note or memorandum of the transaction in existence before the contract is sought to be enforced. It must be signed by the party to be made liable or by some other person lawfully authorised by him. For the purpose of the latter the contract may be enforceable where the person authorised signs only in an agency capacity; *The Maria D*, HL, 1991.

Section 4 of the Statute of Frauds provides that a "promise to answer for the debt, default or miscarriage of another person" must be evidenced in writing. The section refers to a promise by one party to answer for the contractual (or tortious) liability of another. For example, suppose A (the principal debtor) owes money to B (the creditor). If a third party C, promises to pay the debt to B, if A fails to pay, C acts as guarantor of A's liability. The contract is one of guarantee and therefore caught by s.4. If, however, the third party C makes his promise to the principal debtor A, the transaction will not be a contract of guarantee; *Eastwood v Kenyon* (1840).

A contract of guarantee must be distinguished from a contract of indemnity, which is not caught by s.4. In a contract of indemnity, C takes over the liability of A and A is discharged, thus in *Goodman v Chase* (1818), C obtained the debtor A's release from custody by orally promising the sheriff B, that he, C, would pay A's debt. C having assumed primary liability, it was held that the transaction was an (enforceable) indemnity.

Where there has never been a debt between A and B, C's promise cannot be in the nature of a guarantee; *Lakeman v Mounstephen*, HL, 1874.

Exceptional cases

A contract of guarantee only comes within s.4 if it stands on its own. The following exceptions (i.e. cases where there is no requirement of written evidence) are established.

1. Guarantee forms part of a larger transaction. In *Sutton v Grey* (1894), Grey agreed to introduce clients to a firm of stockbrokers. It was orally agreed that Grey should have half the commission earned as a result of the introductions and that he would be liable for half of any loss caused by the default of clients. It was held that although the latter promise was a guarantee, it did not come within s.4 as it formed part of a larger transaction.

2. Guarantee given to release property from liability.
In *Fitzgerald v Dressler* (1859), B sold linseed to A, who resold at a higher price to C. B remained in possession of the goods under a lien until he received payment from A. In order to obtain immediate possession of the goods, C undertook to guarantee A's debt to B. It was held that the transaction was outside s.4.

In order to fall within this exception, the guarantor must be the substantial owner of the property in respect of which the guarantee is given. In *Harburg India Rubber Comb Co v Martin*, CA, 1902, a promise given by a shareholder to guarantee the company's debts did not fall within the exception.

3. Consumer Protection (Distance Selling) Regulations 2000. Another example of legislation prescribing contractual formalities is the Distance Selling Regulations. The regulations apply to "distance contracts", that is;

> "any contract concerning goods or services concluded between a seller and consumer under an organised distance sales or service provision scheme run by the supplier who, for the purposes of the contract, makes exclusive use of one or more means of distance communication up to and including the moment when the contract is concluded" (reg.3(1)).

Schedule 1 of the regulations contains a list of methods of distance communication to which the regulations apply, including: letter; press advertising with order forms; catalogue; telephone; radio; videophone; e-mail; fax; internet; and teleshopping.

The regulations require certain information to be given to the consumer prior to the conclusion of the contract, including the identity of the supplier; a description of the goods and services; the price; delivery costs; and the existence of a right of cancellation (reg.7(1)). The supplier must ensure that this information is given in a form appropriate to the form of distance communication used (reg.7(2)).

Regulation 8 requires the supplier to confirm in writing, or another durable medium (e.g. email), the information already given and also some additional information, including information on the right to cancel the contract. There is a "cooling off period" (i.e. right to cancel) of seven working days from the day after the date of the contract in the case of services, or from the day after the date of delivery of the goods. Where the supplier fails to comply with the information requirement at all, the cooling off period is extended to three months (regs 10–12).

Under reg.5 certain contracts are excluded from the regulations, including: sales of land and construction agreements (other than rental agreements); financial services; contracts concluded by automated machines, via public pay phones and at auction.

6. TERMS OF THE CONTRACT

Contracts consist of various statements, promises, stipulations, etc. grouped together under the word "terms". The terms may be express or implied. It is the terms of the contract which determine the extent of each party's rights and duties and the remedies available if the terms are broken are determined by the comparative importance of the terms.

CERTAINTY

A contract may be void if the terms are not reasonably certain. In *Scammell v Ouston*, HL, 1941, the House of Lords held an arrangement to acquire a van "on hire-purchase terms" too vague to be an enforceable contract.

In commercial transactions, the court may be prepared to enforce an ostensibly vague agreement by reference to trade custom or any previous dealings between the parties; *Hillas Co Ltd v Arcos Ltd*, HL, 1932. Where a contract for the sale of goods does not fix a price, the Sale of Goods Act 1979, s.8 provides that a reasonable price must be paid. It is possible that the parties themselves may provide the machinery for resolving an apparently uncertain term, such as where the price of land is to be fixed by valuers appointed by the parties; *Sudbrook Trading Estate Ltd v Eggleton*, HL, 1982. The *Sudbrook* case was distinguished in *Gillatt v Sky Television Ltd*, CA, 2000. In that case the contract provided that the value of shares was to be determined by an independent chartered accountant. The Court of Appeal held that the appointment of an accountant was not merely a mechanism or permissive procedure, but an essential condition precedent to the existence of any entitlement under the contract.

If an uncertain term is actually meaningless, then exceptionally the court may be prepared to sever the provision if it is clearly superfluous. In *Nicolene Ltd v Simmonds*, CA, 1953, a contract for the sale of goods contained the words, "I assume . . . that the usual conditions of acceptance apply". As there were no usual conditions of acceptance, the Court of Appeal held the words were meaningless and could be ignored.

Although it has always been recognised that an agreement to negotiate will not be valid because it lacks certainty, in *Walford v Miles*, HL, 1992 the validity of so-called "lock-out" agreements was recognised. In such a case, one party agrees that for a specified period he will not negotiate with anyone except the other party. Such an agreement should, of course, be supported by consideration and contain a term specifying the duration of the agreement.

THE PAROL EVIDENCE RULE

There is a general rule, the "parol evidence rule," that where a contract is embodied in a written document, then extrinsic (parol) evidence is not admissible to add to, vary, subtract from or contradict the terms of the written document. Extrinsic evidence is not confined to oral statements but can extend to written matter such as draft contracts and correspondence. The inconvenience and injustice of the rule is obvious and the courts have evaded it by creating a number of exceptions. The Law Commission (1976) have recommended that the rule be abolished.

The main exceptions to the parol evidence rule are as follows:

(1) Custom. Evidence of the customs of a locality or trade usage can be admitted to add to, but not contradict, a written agreement; *Palgrave Brown and Son Ltd v SS. Turid*, HL, 1922.

(2) Operation of the contract. Extrinsic evidence is permissible to show that the contract has not yet come into operation or has ceased to operate. In *Pym v Campbell* (1856), there was a written agreement for the sale of a share in a patent but the parties orally agreed that the agreement was not to operate until a third party approved the invention. Evidence of the oral agreement was admitted.

(3) Validity. Extrinsic evidence is admissible to show that the contract is invalid for mistake, misrepresentation, incapacity or want of consideration.

(4) Evidence as to supplementary terms. There is a presumption that where the contract is reduced to writing, the writing is intended to include all the terms of the contract. This presumption may be rebutted by showing that the contract is partly written and partly oral; *Walker Property Investments Ltd v Walker*, CA, 1947.

(5) Rectification. The equitable remedy of rectification is an exception to the parol evidence rule (see Chapter 9).

(6) Collateral contract. Extrinsic evidence of a collateral contract is admissible; *City of Westminster Properties Ltd v
Mudd* (1959). Collateral contracts are discussed below,
under "Representations and Terms".

REPRESENTATIONS AND TERMS

Statements made by the parties in the course of negotiations
leading up to the formation of the contract are classified by the
court as either representations or terms. A representation is a
statement which induces the contract but does not form part of
it, whereas a term is a promise or undertaking that is part of the
contract itself. If a representation proves false, the remedy will
lie in an action for misrepresentation (see Chapter 8), whereas if
a term is broken the remedy will lie in an action for breach of
contract (see below). In some cases, a misrepresentation later
becomes incorporated into the contract as a term. In such a case
the injured party will have two causes of action: one for
misrepresentation and the other for breach.

Whether a statement is a representation or a term is primarily
a question of intention. If the parties have indicated that a
statement is to be regarded as a term, the court will implement
their intention. In other cases, the following guidelines may be
applied:

Manner and timing of statement

A statement is not likely to be a term if the person making the
statement asks the other party to check or verify it, as where the
seller of a boat stated that it was sound but asked the buyer to
have it surveyed; *Ecay v Godfrey* (1947). If the statement is made
with the intention of preventing the other from finding a defect,
and succeeds in this, the court may consider it to be a term.
Thus, in *Schawel v Reade*, HL, 1913, the vendor of a horse said to
the buyer, "you need not look for anything, the horse is
perfectly sound" and the House of Lords held that the statement was a term. Where there is a distinct interval of time
between the making of the statement and the conclusion of the
contract, this may indicate that the parties do not intend the
statement to be a term; *Routledge v McKay*, CA, 1954. In the
recent case of *Inntrepreneur Pub Co v East Crown Ltd* (2000),
Lightman J. said that the longer the interval between the
statement and the contract, "the greater the presumption must

be that the parties did not intend the statement to have contractual effect".

Importance of statement

A statement is likely to be a term if it is such that the injured party would not have entered into the contract had it not been made. In *Bannerman v White* (1861), a prospective purchaser of hops asked whether they had been treated with sulphur, adding that if they had, he would not even trouble to ask the price. The seller's (erroneous) statement that sulphur had not been used was held to be a term.

Special knowledge and skill

Where one of the parties possesses superior knowledge and skill relating to the subject-matter, the court may conclude that any statement made by such a party is a term. In *Dick Bentley Productions Ltd v Harold Smith (Motors) Ltd*, CA, 1965, a car dealer gave a false statement as to the mileage of a Bentley. The Court of Appeal held the dealer's statement to be a term, thus distinguishing *Oscar Chess Ltd v Williams*, CA, 1957 where, on a part-exchange deal, a private car owner falsely (but honestly) stated the age of the car to the dealer. The statement was held to be a representation; the dealer was in at least as strong a position to verify the truth of the statement.

Statement reduced to writing

Where the agreement has been reduced to a written document, statements appearing in the written contract will normally be regarded as terms. Subject to the matters discussed above, statements excluded from the written contract are likely to be regarded as representations. Nevertheless, the court will look to the intention of the parties to see whether they intended a contract partly written and partly oral; *J. Evans and Son (Portsmouth) Ltd v Andrea Merzario Ltd*, CA, 1976.

It may be possible to avoid the argument that a contract is partly written and partly oral by the insertion of an "entire agreement" clause in the written contract. Such a clause states that the written document is intended and agreed to contain the entirety of the contract, each party acknowledging that they have not relied on any representation or statement not contained in the written document.

COLLATERAL CONTRACTS

Where a contract is entered into on the faith of a statement made by one of the parties, there may be a secondary or "collateral" contract based upon the statement.

In *De Lassalle v Guildford*, CA, 1901, the defendant was negotiating the lease of a house to the claimant, who refused to complete unless the defendant orally assured him that the drains were in order. The defendant gave such an assurance, but no term to that effect was inserted into the lease document. The drains were not in order and the claimant sued for damages not upon the lease (which did not refer to the drains), but on a collateral contract based on the defendant's oral assurance. The consideration to enforce this promise as a separate contract was the claimant's execution of the lease, i.e. his entering into the main contract.

The following points should be noted in connection with collateral contracts:

(1) Although the collateral contract is essentially a judicial device, the court will not find such a contract unless all the elements of a separate valid contract are present; *Heilbut, Symons Co v Buckleton*, HL, 1913.

(2) A collateral contract may be valid even though it conflicts with a term in the main contract. In *City of Westminster Properties Ltd v Mudd* (1959), a lease contained a covenant that the premises should only be used for business. The tenant residing there was only induced to sign the lease by an oral assurance by the landlord that he could continue to do so. It was held that the oral assurance formed the basis of a collateral contract which could be raised as a defence in an action for breach of covenant by the landlord.

(3) The collateral contract device proved useful in circumventing the rule that damages were not available for non-fraudulent misrepresentation. Since damages are now available for such misrepresentation (see Chapter 8), the device has lost some of its significance. It may, however, be used to side-step the parol evidence rule and has been used in certain other contexts, e.g. to evade an exclusion clause (see Chapter 7) and to avoid the effects of an illegal contract (see Chapter 11). The decision in *Record v Bell* (1991) shows that the collateral contract device can be

relied upon in certain circumstances to get round s.2 of the Law of Property (Miscellaneous Provisions) Act 1989 (see above). In that case it was held that although the correspondence did not satisfy s.2, a letter by the vendor offering a warranty as to title, intended to induce the purchaser to exchange, amounted to an enforceable collateral contract when accepted by the exchange of contracts. See also *Shanklin Pier Ltd v Detel Products Ltd* (1951), discussed in Chapter 12.

(4) In the *Inntrepreneur* case (see above) it was held (following *Deepak Fertilisers and Petrochemical Corp v Davy McKee (London) Ltd* (1999)) that an entire agreement clause in an agreement for a lease of a public house precluded the tenant setting up a collateral contract as a defence to an action for breach of contract.

CONDITIONS, WARRANTIES AND INNOMINATE TERMS

Not all the terms of the contract are of equal importance and the law has sought to classify them according to their importance. The normal classification is into conditions, warranties and innominate terms.

Condition

The word "condition" may be used to denote a condition precedent or condition subsequent (i.e. events upon which the existence of the contract depends; see *Pym v Campbell* (1856) and *Head v Tattersall* (1871)), but it is most commonly used to describe an important term of the contract. The breach of a condition will entitle the injured party to treat himself as discharged from the contract as well as giving him the right to sue for damages.

Warranty

The word "warranty" is commonly used to denote a contractual term of lesser importance, the breach of which gives the injured party the right to claim damages only and not to treat himself as discharged from the contract.

Whether a term is a condition or a warranty depends on the intention of the parties. A neat illustration of the distinction is to be found by contrasting *Poussard v Spiers* (1876) (condition) and

Bettini v Gye (1876) (warranty). In *Poussard* an opera singer's obligation to sing on the first night of a three month series of concerts was held to be a condition; in *Bettini*, the singer's obligation to attend all the rehearsals was held to be a warranty.

The fact that the parties have described a term in the contract as a "condition" is not conclusive if in fact it is a warranty, and vice versa; *L. Schuler A.G. v Wickman Machine Tool Sales Ltd*, HL, 1974. In that case the contract stated that it was "a condition of this agreement" that the defendants should make 1,400 visits to six named car companies over a four and a half year period. A majority of the House of Lords did not accept that the failure to make one visit should entitle the other party to terminate the contract. The parties could not have intended the term to operate as a condition in circumstances where it produced such an unreasonable result. This approach was followed in *Rice v Great Yarmouth Borough Council*, CA, 2000, where there was a clause in a long term leisure management agreement that "if the contractor committed a breach of any of its obligations under the contract . . . the council . . . may terminate [the contract]". The Court of Appeal held that the clause could not have been intended by the parties to apply to minor breaches, but only those giving rise to a right to terminate the contract.

Innominate term

The above definitions of conditions and warranties derive from the Sale of Goods Act 1893 (now enacted in the Sale of Goods Act 1979) but came to be applied by the courts to other types of contract apart from the sale of goods. The classification is based upon an examination of the contract itself to ascertain whether the parties intended a particular term to be a condition or a warranty. It has the merit of certainty in that the consequences of a breach (termination or damages) may be predicted in advance.

More recently the courts have looked at the effect of a breach on the injured party to ascertain whether a condition or a warranty has been broken. A term will be classed as "innominate" where it is only when the effects of its breach are considered that its true nature is revealed. The merit of this approach is flexibility.

A leading case on the innominate approach is *Hong Kong Fir Shipping Co Ltd v Kawasaki Kisen Kaisha Ltd*, CA, 1962 in which the defendants chartered a ship from the claimants for a period of two years. The engines were antiquated and the staff incompetent with the result that 20 weeks were lost. The defendants repudiated the charter alleging breach of a "condition" to provide a seaworthy ship. The claimants brought an action for wrongful repudiation, arguing that their breach was not such as entitled the defendants to terminate the contract, but only to claim damages. The Court of Appeal found for the claimants; the question to be asked was whether, looking at the events which had occurred as a result of the breach, the defendants had been deprived of the whole of the benefit to which they were entitled under the contract. The Court of Appeal answered the question in the negative; the breach was not such as justified termination.

Despite modern judicial reluctance to classify terms as conditions or warranties, the courts are still prepared to do so if the circumstances require it. In *The Mihalis Angelos*, CA, 1971, it was held that a clause in a charter party that a ship would be ready to load on a certain date was a condition, and in *Bunge Corp v Tradax S.A.*, HL, 1981, the House of Lords arrived at a similar decision concerning the time-table in a contract of sale. Nevertheless, in *The Hansa Nord*, CA, 1975 the Court of Appeal said that it was wrong to assume, even in a contract governed by the Sale of Goods Act, that a term was either a condition or a warranty. It was possible to have an "intermediate" (innominate) term, where the remedy for breach (termination or damages) would depend upon the nature of the breach.

IMPLIED TERMS

There are three ways in which terms which have not been expressed may be implied into the contract: by the court, by custom and by statute.

Terms implied by the court

Where a term is not expressly stated, but is one which the parties, in the view of the court, must have intended to include in order to give the contract business efficacy, the term may be implied into the contract. Such a term must be:

> "something so obvious that it goes without saying; so that, if while the parties were making their bargain, an officious bystander were to suggest some express provision for it in the agreement, they would testily suppress him with a common 'oh of course!'" *Shirlaw v Southern Foundries Ltd*, CA, 1939.

An example of an implied term is *The Moorcock* (CA, 1889), where the defendants, wharf-owners, agreed to allow the plaintiffs to unload a vessel. The vessel grounded at low tide and was damaged. Despite the absence of an express term, the defendants were held liable for breach of an implied term to take reasonable care that the berth was safe. The implied term was necessary in order to give the contract efficacy.

A term cannot be implied where one of the parties has no knowledge of the matter to be implied; *Spring v National Amalgamated Stevedores and Dockers Society* (1956). It is also the case that there can be no implication of a term to which one party would clearly have not agreed; *National Bank of Greece S.A. v Pinios Shipping Co*, CA, 1989. Terms implied under this test are something of a rarity; it is irrelevant that the term which is sought to be implied would make the contract more reasonable; *Liverpool C.C. v Irwin*, HL, 1977.

A term may also be implied by the court, not according to the parties' intentions, but as a matter of law. Many of these implied terms are well-established in the law concerning particular types of contract, such as master and servant, landlord and tenant. Thus, in *Liverpool C.C. v Irwin*, the House of Lords held that it was an implied term in a tenancy agreement of a council flat that the landlord should take reasonable care to keep lifts and staircases in a reasonable state of repair. The law is as yet unclear as to whether the test for implying such terms is based on reasonableness or necessity. It should be noted that many such terms have been incorporated into statutes, e.g. S.G.A. 1979; the Supply of Goods and Services Act 1982.

In *Johnson v Unisys Ltd*, HL, 2001, an employer summarily dismissed the claimant who obtained compensation for unfair dismissal from an employment tribunal. The claimant sought a much greater sum by way of civil damages. The claimant contended that there was an implied term that the employer would not exercise its right except for good cause and after giving the claimant the chance to demonstrate that there was no such cause. This contention was based on *Malik v Bank of Credit and Commerce International SA (in liquidation)*, HL, 2000 (see Chapter 14). A majority of the House of Lords held that the existence of statutory machinery providing compensation precluded the court from implying the term.

Terms implied by custom

Terms may be implied into a contract by adducing evidence of local custom or trade usage with respect to matters upon which the contract is silent; *Hutton v Warren* (1836). A custom will not be implied if it is contrary to the express terms of the contract; *Les Affréteurs Réunis S.A. v Walford* (HL, 1919).

Terms implied by statute

Certain statutes imply terms into particular types of contract. A recent example of a statute which implies terms into contracts is the Late Payment of Commercial Debts (Interest) Act 1998. Where it applies, the Act provides for an implied term that any qualifying debt carries interest; however, the Act may be excluded in certain situations. Of particular importance are the terms implied by the Sale of Goods Act 1979 (as amended by the Sale and Supply of Goods Act 1994) into contracts for the sale of goods. In essence, the implied terms are as follows:

(1) Title. There is an implied condition that a seller has the right to sell the goods and implied warranties that the goods are free from incumbrances and that the buyer will enjoy quiet possession (s.12).
(2) Description. There is an implied condition that the goods will correspond with the description (s.13).
(3) Fitness for purpose and satisfactory quality. Where goods are sold in the course of a business, there is an implied condition that the goods shall be reasonably fit for the purpose for which they are required and an implied term that the goods shall be of satisfactory quality (s.14).
(4) Sale by sample. In such a sale, there are various implied conditions including a condition that the bulk correspond with the sample in quality (s.15).

There are similar statutory implied terms in contracts of hire-purchase and contracts for the supply of goods. The extent to which such implied terms may be excluded by the parties is considered in Chapter 7.

7. EXCLUSION CLAUSES

A clause may be inserted into a contract which purports to exclude (or financially limit) one party's liability for breach of contract, misrepresentation or negligence.

Historically, the courts have sought by various means to control the use of such clauses and latterly Parliament has intervened, most notably with the Unfair Contract Terms Act 1977 and the Unfair Terms in Consumer Contracts Regulations 1999.

Control by the courts has proceeded on two broad fronts; the defendant may only rely on an exclusion clause if it has been incorporated into the contract, and if, as a matter of construction, it extends to the loss in question. These matters are considered below.

INCORPORATION

Document signed

If the plaintiff signs a document purporting to have contractual effect containing an exclusion clause, he is bound by its terms. This is so even if he has not read the document and regardless of whether he understands it or not; *L'Estrange v Graucob*, CA, 1934. However, even a signed document can be rendered wholly or partly ineffective by a misrepresentation as to its effect; in *Curtis v Chemical Cleaning and Dyeing Co Ltd*, CA, 1951 the claimant took a dress to be cleaned. She was induced to sign a document which she was told excluded the defendant's liability for damage to sequins. In fact, the document excluded liability for any damage. The dress was returned stained and it was held that the defendants were not protected by the clause which would only protect them in the event of damage to sequins.

The requirement of notice

Where the document is unsigned but merely delivered to the other party, then reasonable and sufficient notice of the existence of the exclusion clause must be given.

For this requirement to be satisfied, (i) the clause must be contained in a contractual document, i.e. one which the reasonable person would assume to contain contractual terms, and not in a document which merely acknowledges payment, such as a voucher or receipt (*Chapelton v Barry* U.D.C. (1940)); and (ii) the existence of the exclusion clause must be brought to the notice of the other party before or at the time the contract is entered into. Thus, in *Olley v Marlborough Court*, CA, 1949, the claimant arrived at an hotel and paid for a room at reception. It was held that a notice in the bedroom containing an exclusion clause was not incorporated; since the contract was formed at reception, the notice came too late to affect the claimant's rights.

In fact, the courts require that notice of the exclusion clause should be reasonably contemporaneous with the formation of the contract, although where the document is issued by an automatic machine, the Court of Appeal has taken a strict view. In *Thornton v Shoe Lane Parking Ltd*, CA, 1971, Lord Denning M.R. decided that conditions on a ticket issued by an automatic car park barrier came too late; the contract had been concluded a moment before when the claimant placed his vehicle on the spot which activated the barrier.

It should be noted that reasonable, not actual, notice is required. What is reasonable is a question of fact depending on all the circumstances and the situation of the parties; it may depend on the category or class of persons to which the claimant belongs. In *Thompson v L.M.S. Railway Co* (1930), an illiterate railway passenger was held bound by a clause since sufficient notice had been given to the ordinary railway traveller. In a long line of so-called "ticket cases," the courts repeatedly held that attention should be drawn to the existence of excluding terms by clear words on the front of any document delivered to the claimant, e.g. "for conditions, see back".

It seems that the degree of notice required may increase according to the gravity or unusualness of the clause in question; *Thornton v Shoe Lane Parking Ltd*, CA, 1971. It is clear from *Interfoto Picture Library Ltd v Stiletto Visual Programmes Ltd*, CA, 1988 that this requirement applies to unusual contract terms generally and not merely to exclusion clauses.

Previous dealings

Even where there has been insufficient notice, an exclusion clause may nevertheless be incorporated where there has been a previous course of dealing between the parties on the same terms; *J. Spurling Ltd v Bradshaw*, CA, 1956. Thus, the claimant in

Olley v Marlborough Court (above) might well have been bound by the clause if she had stayed at the hotel many times before. The previous course of dealing must have been consistent (*McCutcheon v David MacBrayne Ltd* (HL, 1964)) and it seems that knowledge of the existence of the clause on the part of the claimant (as opposed to its content) will suffice in order to bind the claimant by a previous course of dealing; *Hardwick Game Farm Ltd v Suffolk Agricultural Producer Association*, HL, 1969. As against a consumer, a considerable number of past transactions may be required; *Hollier v Rambler Motors (AMC) Ltd*, CA, 1972.

A course of dealing was established in *Petrotrade Inc v Texaco Ltd*, CA, 2000. The parties had orally agreed the sale of a cargo and later the claimant sent a telex to the defendant confirming the contract and setting out some additional terms and conditions. The claimant contended that these terms were incorporated on the basis of 22 previous transactions in the previous 12 months on the same terms. The Court of Appeal held that the terms were indeed incorporated.

CONSTRUCTION

Once it is established that an exclusion clause is incorporated, the whole contract will be construed (i.e. interpreted) to see whether the clause covers the breach that has occurred. The basic approach is that liability can only be excluded by clear words. The rules of construction should not be applied as strictly to limitation clauses as to exclusion clauses; *Ailsa Craig Fishing Co Ltd v Malvern Fishing Co Ltd*, HL, 1983. The main rules of construction are as follows:

Contra proferentem rule

Under this rule, any ambiguity in the wording of an exclusion clause will be construed as narrowly as possible against the party purporting to rely on the clause. Thus, in *Houghton v Trafalgar Insurance Co*, CA, 1954, a car insurance policy excluded the insurer's liability where an excessive "load" was being carried. It was held that the clause did not extend to the situation where a car was carrying an excess of passengers, the word "load" being narrowly construed as referring to goods, not people.

Where it is sought to exclude liability for negligence, particularly clear words are required; *Smith v South Wales Switchgear Ltd*, HL, 1978. The principles are as follows:

(1) If the clause expressly refers to negligence, or uses some synonym for negligence, it will be effective.

(2) In the absence of such express reference, if the words are wide enough to cover negligence the clause may nevertheless be effective, unless there is some liability other than negligence to which the words would apply.

In *White v John Warwick Co Ltd*, CA, 1953, the claimant was injured riding a cycle hired from the defendants, under a clause stating that "nothing in this agreement shall render the owners liable for personal injury". In supplying the defective cycle, the defendants could have been held liable for both breach of contract and negligence. The Court of Appeal held that the clause was ambiguous and construed it to refer to the defendants' contractual liability and so the defendants were not protected if they were found to be negligent. By contrast, in *Alderslade v Hendon Laundry Ltd*, CA, 1945, the claimant sent articles for laundering which were then lost. The Court of Appeal held that a limitation clause referring to "lost or damaged" articles must apply to negligence since if it did not apply to negligence, it would be redundant (the launderers' only liability in relation to the safe custody of the articles was in negligence).

The above rules are rules of construction only and will not be applied rigidly to defeat the intentions of the parties. Thus, in *Lamport and Holt Lines Ltd v Cambro and Scrutton Ltd*, CA, 1982, during a refit of the claimant's ship, a derrick collapsed through the defendants' negligence. An exclusion clause referring to damage arising from "any act or omission" was held to be sufficiently wide to embrace negligence, despite the absence of any express reference to, or synonym for, negligence.

Repugnance to main purpose

In some cases an exclusion clause has been struck down by applying a presumption of construction that the clause is not intended to defeat the main purpose of the contract; *Glynn v Margetson*, HL, 1893. For example, in *Sze Hai Tong Bank Ltd v Rambler Cycle Co Ltd* (PC, 1959), goods were shipped under a clause providing that the responsibility of the carrier should cease absolutely after the goods had been discharged from the ship. It was held that the clause must be modified so as to prevent reliance where the goods were knowingly delivered to a party not entitled to receive them, since this would defeat the main purpose of the contract. Although the main purpose rule was endorsed by the House of Lords in the *Suisse Atlantique* case (see below), its role is now unclear in view of the modern tendency to construe the whole contract (rather than the exclusion clause in isolation) and the fact that where the Unfair Contract Terms Act applies (see below), such a clause must in any case satisfy the requirement of reasonableness.

Fundamental breach

In the 1950s and 1960s, the courts, building on earlier decisions, developed a doctrine that, as a rule of law, an exclusion clause could not protect a party from liability for a serious, i.e. fundamental, breach of contract, even where, on its true construction, the wording of the clause covered the breach which had occurred. The so-called "doctrine of fundamental breach" was rejected by the House of Lords in *Suisse Atlantique Société d'Armement Maritime S.A. v N.V. Rotterdamsche Kolen Centrale* (HL, 1967) who stated, *obiter*, that there was no rule of substantive law that an exclusion clause could not cover a fundamental breach; it was a question of construction whether the clause in fact covered the breach in question.

The Court of Appeal effectively revived the rule of law doctrine in *Harbutt's "Plasticine" Ltd v Wayne Tank and Pump Co Ltd, CA*, 1970 and subsequent cases, albeit in a modified form. In 1980, *Harbutt* and the cases which followed it were overruled by the House of Lords in *Photo Production Ltd v Securicor Transport Ltd*, HL, 1980, which reaffirmed *Suisse Atlantique*.

In *Photo Production*, the claimants employed the defendants to protect their factory by a visiting patrol. A clause provided that "under no circumstances shall the (defendant) company be responsible for any injurious act or default by any employee of the company". One night, one of the defendants' guards lit a small fire inside the factory which got out of control and completely destroyed the claimant's premises, with loss amounting to £615,000. The House of Lords held that though the defendants were in breach, they were permitted to rely on the clause as it clearly and unambiguously covered the breach in question.

Although the Unfair Contract Terms Act did not apply to the case (the facts occurred before the Act came into force), the decision is clearly also based on the reasonableness of the clause since the parties, being of equal bargaining power, were free to apportion the risks as they thought fit. The claimants, as owners of the premises, were in a better position to insure against the risk of fire. The decision in *Photo Production* is in line with s.9(1) of the Unfair Contract Terms Act (see below).

FURTHER LIMITATIONS ON EXCLUSION CLAUSES

Position of third parties

As a result of the doctrine of privity (see Chapter 12), historically the courts have held a person who is not a party to contract (a third party) is not protected by an exclusion clause in that contract, even if the clause purports to extend to him. Employees are regarded in this context as third parties; thus in *Cosgrove v Horsfall*, CA, 1945 a bus passenger was travelling under a free pass containing a clause that neither the bus authority nor its servants would be liable for injury. The passenger was injured as a result of the negligence of the bus driver. The driver was held liable in negligence as he was not a party to the contract containing the exclusion clause.

The decision was affirmed by the House of Lords in *Scruttons Ltd v Midland Silicones Ltd*, HL, 1962. Here a contract for the carriage of a drum of chemicals from the United States to England contained a clause limiting the liability of the carriers to $500. The drum was damaged through the negligence of a firm of stevedores whom the carriers had employed to unload the ship. It was held that the stevedores could not rely on the limitations clause contained in the contract between the carriers and the owners of the drum, to which they were not a party. The House also held that the stevedores could not rely on a similar limitation clause in the contract between the carriers and themselves, to which the owners were not a party.

The decision in *Scruttons* was avoided by the *Privy Council in N.Z. Shipping Co Ltd v A.M. Satterthwaite Co Ltd*, PC, 1975. Here it was held that the stevedore may take the benefit of the exclusion clause in a contract of carriage providing certain conditions are satisfied:

(1) the contract of carriage must make it clear that the stevedore is intended to be protected by the exclusion clause;

(2) the contract of carriage must make it clear that the carrier is contracting both on his own behalf and as agent for the stevedore;

(3) the stevedore must have authorised the carrier to contract in this way; and

(4) the stevedore must have provided consideration for the promise to exclude his liability.

In *Satterthwaite*, the consideration was held to consist in unloading the goods, which constituted the performance of an existing contractual duty owed to a third party, applying *Scotson v Pegg* (see Chapter 4). However, the somewhat elaborate device relied on in *Satterthwaite* may no longer be necessary now that the provisions of the Contracts (Rights of Third Parties) Act are in force (see Chapter 12). This permits the parties to contract on the basis that a third party may take the benefit of an exclusion clause.

Another inroad into the position established by the *Scruttons* case is to be seen in *Norwich City Council v Harvey*, CA, 1989. Building owners employed the main contractors to construct an extension to a swimming pool. A clause in the standard form contract provided that the risk of fire damage should be upon the owners and required them to maintain adequate insurance. The contractors sub-contracted certain work; the sub-contract referred to the clause in the main contract and stated that it would apply. The defendant, an employee of the sub-contractors, negligently damaged the building by fire. An action by the owners against the defendant failed on the basis that no duty of care was owed to the owners who were taken to have assumed the risk of fire damage.

Inconsistent oral promise

An exclusion clause may be rendered wholly or partly ineffective by an inconsistent oral promise. In *Mendelssohn v Normand Ltd*, CA, 1970, an oral statement by a garage attendant that the claimant should leave his car unlocked was held to override an exclusion clause relating to non-liability for goods stolen. The defendant garage was held not to be protected by the clause when valuables were stolen from the claimant's car.

In some cases, the court has treated the inconsistent oral promise as forming the basis of a collateral contract. Thus, in *Webster v Higgin*, CA, 1948, an oral promise by a dealer that a car was in good condition was held to be enforceable as a collateral contract despite the fact that the hire-purchase contract (the main contract) contained an exclusion clause. (For collateral contracts, see Chapter 6.)

LEGISLATION

The first major attempt to control exclusion clauses in contract generally came with s.3 of the Misrepresentation Act 1967 (now re-enacted in the Unfair Contract Terms Act, s.8), followed by the Supply of Goods (Implied Terms) Act 1973 (now re-enacted in the Unfair Contract Terms Act, s.6). The basic purpose of the Unfair Contract Terms Act, which was passed in 1977, is to restrict the extent to which liability in a contract can be excluded for breach of contract and negligence, largely by reference to the reasonableness requirement, but in some cases by a specific prohibition. Additionally, the Fair Trading Act 1973 gave the Government power to make an order, where an exclusion clause is "inequitable", rendering it a criminal offence to continue to use the clause. This was an important measure of consumer protection. Statutory control over unfair terms has been extended by the Unfair Terms in Consumer Contracts Regulations 1999 which give effect to EC Directive 93/13.

The Unfair Contract Terms Act 1977

1. Scope. With the exception of implied terms in sale of goods and hire-purchase contracts (s.6), such terms in supply of goods and services contracts (s.7) and misrepresentation (s.8), the Act applies only to what is termed "business liability". This is defined by s.1(3) as liability arising from things done by a person in the course of a business or from the occupation of business premises. Thus, transactions of a private nature are outside the scope of the Act.

There are certain types of contract to which the Act does not apply; these are listed in Sch. I and include contracts relating to the transfer of an interest in land and contracts of insurance.

2. Negligence. Liability for death or personal injury resulting from negligence cannot be excluded or restricted by any contract term or notice (s.2(1)). Any provision purporting to have this effect is, therefore, invalid. However, the exclusion or restriction of negligence liability for other loss or damage is permissible, but only in so far as the term or notice satisfies the requirement of reasonableness (s.2(2)). (As to "reasonableness," see below.)

3. Contractual liability. Where one party "deals as consumer" or on the other party's written standard terms of business, then the other party cannot exclude or restrict his liability for breach of contract, except subject to the requirement of reasonableness (s.3(2)(a)). The reasonableness requirement is also extended to terms purporting to entitle the other party to render, (i) performance substantially different from that reasonably expected; or (ii) no performance at all (s.3(2)(b)). In *Pegler v Wang* (2000) the only clauses in the contract that were in standard form were the exclusion and limitation clauses themselves. The evidence showed that these clauses were, from the defendant's point of view, non-negotiable. The court held that the claimant had contracted on the defendant's "written standard terms of business" and therefore s.3 applied. It would seem, therefore, that it is not necessary for the contract as a whole to be in standard form, nor will it matter that one of the non-material clauses has been varied; *St Albans City and District Council v International Computers Ltd*, CA, 1996; and *Watford Electronics Ltd v Sanderson CFL Ltd* (2000), at first instance, per Thornton J.

The expression "deals as consumer" is defined in s.12 if the Act (as amended by the Sale and Supply of Goods to Consumers Regulations 2002) as follows:

> "(1) A party to a contract 'deals as consumer' in relation to another party if:
>
> (a) he neither makes the contract in the course of a business nor holds himself out as doing so; and
> (b) the other party does make the contract in the course of a business; and
> (c) in the case of a contract governed by the law of sale of goods or hire purchase, or by s.7, (see below) the goods passing under or in pursuance of the contract are of a type ordinarily supplied for private use and consumption.
>
> (1A) But if the first party mentioned in subsection (1) is an individual para. (c) of that subsection must be ignored.
>
> (2) But the buyer is not in any circumstances to be regarded as dealing as consumer-
>
> (a) if he is an individual and the goods are secondhand goods sold at public auction at which individuals have the opportunity of attending the sale in person;
> (b) if he is not an individual and the goods are sold by auction or competitive tender.
>
> (3) Subject to this, it is for those claiming that a party does not deal as consumer to show that he does."

The courts have given a wide meaning to "consumer" transaction in the context of s.12 of the 1977 Act. In *R & B Customs*

Brokers Co Ltd v United Dominions Trust Ltd, CA, 1988, the Court of Appeal held that a transaction was made in the course of a business where it was integral to the business itself, or, where there was a regularity of such dealings. In the case, a company purchased a car for both business and private use. The Court of Appeal held that the purchaser was dealing as consumer because buying cars was not integral to the company's business nor was there a sufficient regularity of such transactions. The decision has attracted some criticism. Under the Sale of Goods Act 1979, s.14 (see Chapter 6) a sale will be in the course of a business unless it is a purely private transaction; *Stevenson v Rogers*, CA, 1999. Nevertheless, the *R & B Customs* approach appears to have been confirmed in *Feldaroll Foundry Plc v Hermes Leasing*, CA, 2004.

4. Sale of goods and hire-purchase. In contracts for the sale of goods and hire-purchase, the implied terms as to title cannot be excluded or restricted by a contract term. As against a person dealing as consumer, liability for the implied terms as to correspondence with description or sample, fitness for purpose and merchantable quality cannot be excluded by a contract term. As against a person dealing otherwise than as consumer, such liability can only be excluded or restricted in so far as the term satisfies the requirement of reasonableness (s.6). The provisions of s.6 are not confined to business liability but extend to liability arising under any contract of sale or hire-purchase.

There are similar provisions relating to implied terms in contracts for the supply of goods and services in s.7.

5. Affirmation and breach. Notwithstanding that a contract has been terminated by breach or by a party electing to treat it as repudiated, a term which is required to meet the requirement of reasonableness may nevertheless be found to do so and given effect to (s.9(1)). Conversely, where, on a breach, the contract is nevertheless affirmed by a party entitled to treat it as repudiated, this does not, of itself, exclude the requirement of reasonableness in relation to any contract term (s.9(2)).

6. Reasonableness. Where a term must satisfy the requirement of reasonableness, the test is that the term shall have been a fair and reasonable one to be included having regard to the circumstances which were, or ought reasonably to have been, known to, or in the contemplation of, the parties when the contract was made (s.11(1)).

Where the reasonableness requirement must be met in the case of a limitation clause, the court's attention is drawn to, (i) the resources available to meet the liability; and (ii) the extent to which insurance cover was open to the party purporting to limit liability (s.11(4)). No further guidance is provided by the Act except that, in relation to clauses excluding liability for breach of the implied terms in sale of goods, etc. contracts (those governed by ss.6–7) certain guidelines are laid down in Sch. 2. It is clear that these guidelines will be looked at in other types of contract and therefore their importance cannot be underestimated. The guidelines are, so far as appear to the court to be relevant, as follows:

(1) the strength of the bargaining positions of the parties relevant to each other, taking into account the availability of another source of supply;

(2) whether the customer received an inducement to agree to the term, e.g. where goods are offered more cheaply with an exclusion clause but more expensively without; *R.W. Green Ltd v Cade Bros Farms* (1978);

(3) whether the customer ought to have known the existence and extent of the term. This would appear to refer to knowledge and awareness of the clause via trade custom and previous dealings;

(4) where the term excludes or restricts any relevant liability if some condition is not complied with, whether it was reasonable at the time of the contract to expect that compliance with that condition would be practicable. In *Green v Cade*, seed potatoes were delivered on terms that any notice of rejection or complaint must be made within three days after delivery. The clause was held unreasonable in relation to a defect not discoverable on inspection at the time of delivery;

(5) whether the goods were manufactured, processed or adapted to the special order of the customer.

Further judicial guidance as to reasonableness has been provided by *George Mitchell (Chesterhall) Ltd v Finney Lock Seeds Ltd*, HL, 1983 which was decided under the similar provisions of s.55 of the Sale of Goods Act 1979. Lord Bridge, in referring to the trial judge's decision as to whether a clause is reasonable, said:

"There will sometimes be room for legitimate difference of judicial opinion . . . the appellate court should treat the original decision with the utmost respect and refrain from interference with it unless satisfied that it proceeded on some erroneous principle or was plainly and obviously wrong."

In this case, the defendants supplied the claimant farmers with cabbage seed for £201. The contract contained a clause that if the seeds were defective, liability would be limited to the replacement of the seed or refunding the price. The crop failed owing to the seeds being unmerchantable and the claimants suffered loss amounting to £61,000. The House of Lords upheld the unanimous decision of the Court of Appeal that it would not be fair and reasonable to allow reliance on the clause. A recent illustration of the approach of the courts is to be found in *Watford Electronics Ltd v Sanderson CFL Ltd*, CA, 2001. The claimants (W) sought damages from the defendants (S) for breach of a contract to supply computer hardware and software. The contract contained, (a) an entire agreement clause; (b) a clause excluding liability for direct or consequential losses; and (c) a clause limiting liability to the price paid by W under the contract (£104,000). The system installed failed to perform and W sought damages of £5.5 million in respect of loss of profits and other costs. At first instance, Thornton J. held that clauses (b) and (c) were unreasonable in their entirety and fell foul of s.11 of the Unfair Contract Terms Act. The Court of Appeal found that the judge had erred in his approach as clauses (b) and (c) consisted of two distinct terms, in relation to each of which it was necessary to consider whether the reasonableness test was satisfied. Accordingly the judge's decision was reversed and the clauses upheld as reasonable. The Court rejected the judge's finding that clause (b) covered liability for misrepresentation (see Chapter 8). The entire agreement clause prevented that liability from arising.

The Court of Appeal stressed that the contract had been negotiated between experienced businessmen of equal bargaining power and skill. Unless satisfied that one party had effectively taken unfair advantage of the other, or that a term was so unreasonable as plainly not to have been understood or considered, the court should not interfere (per Chadwick L.J.).

Gibson L.J. adopted the dictum of Forbes J. in *Salvage Association v CAP Financial Services* (1995) where he said:

"Generally speaking, where a party well able to look after itself enters into a commercial contract and, with full knowledge of all relevant circumstances, willingly accepts the terms of the contract which provides for apportionment of the financial risks of that transaction, I think it is very likely that those terms will be held to be fair and reasonable."

Unfair Terms in Consumer Contract Regulations 1999

The EC Directive on Unfair Terms in Consumer Contracts (Directive 93/13) was originally transposed into domestic legislation by the Unfair Terms in Consumer Contracts Regulations 1994. These regulations have now been replaced by the 1999 regulations which came into force on October 1, 1999.

1. Scope. The regulations apply to unfair terms in contracts concluded between a seller or a supplier and a consumer (reg.4(1)). A consumer is a "natural person who is acting for purposes which are outside his trade, business or profession".

2. Effect. An unfair term shall not be binding on the consumer; however the contract shall continue to bind the parties if capable of existing without the unfair term (regs 8(1) and 8(2)). The assessment of unfairness will take into account all the circumstances attending the conclusion of the contract (reg.6(1)).

A contractual term which has not been individually negotiated shall be regarded as unfair if, contrary to the requirement of good faith, it causes a significant imbalance in the parties' rights and obligations to the detriment of the consumer (reg.5(1)). A term will be regarded as "not individually negotiated" if drafted in the advance and so the consumer has not been able to influence the substance of the term (reg.5(2)). However, even where a specific term has been negotiated, this will not prevent the regulations applying to the rest of the contract if, overall, it is a pre-formulated standard form of contract (reg.5(3)).

The burden of proving that a term was individually negotiated falls on the seller or supplier (reg.5(4)).

Schedule 2 to the regulations contains an "indicative and non-exhaustive list" of seventeen terms which may be regarded as unfair.

The examples in the list include the following:

(1) excluding or limiting the legal liability of a seller or supplier in the event of the death of a consumer or personal injury to the latter resulting from an act or omission of that seller or supplier (Sch.2.1 (a));

(2) making the agreement binding on the consumer whereas provision of services by the seller or supplier is subject to a condition whose realisation depends on his will alone (Sch.2.1 (c));

(3) requiring any consumer who fails to fulfil his obligation to pay a disproportionately high sum in compensation (Sch.2.1(e));

(4) obliging the consumer to fulfil all his obligations where the seller or supplier does not perform his (Sch.2.1(o)).

3. Written contracts. A seller or supplier must ensure that any written term is expressed in plain, intelligible language (reg.7(1)).

4. Main subject matter and price. In so far as it is in plain, intelligible language, no assessment shall be made of the fairness of any term which relates to the definition of the main subject matter of the contract or the adequacy of the price or remuneration as against the goods or services supplied (reg.6(2)). It seems that reg.6(2) is to be given a restrictive interpretation: *Bairstow Eves London Central Ltd v Smith*, 2004.

5. Supervision. Regulation 10 provides that the Director General of Fair Trading shall consider any complaint made to him about the fairness of any contract term drawn up for general use. He may seek an injunction restraining the use of an unfair term.

The regulations provide for the first time that certain qualifying bodies named in Sch.1 of the regulations may also apply for an injunction to prevent the continued use of an unfair term; they must, however, notify the Director General of their intention (reg.12)). These qualifying bodies include (for some purposes) the Consumers' Association; also trading standards departments and statutory regulators. In addition, the regulations provide for an enhanced role for the Director General and also the qualifying bodies in the supervision and control of unfair terms in general use (regs 13—15).

An action commenced by the Director General came before the House of Lords in *Director General of Fair Trading v First National Bank*, HL, 2001. The case concerned a term in the Bank's standard form loan agreement. The term provided that, where the borrower was in default and the Bank had obtained a court judgment for the amount due, interest at the contract rate continued to be payable until the judgment was discharged, despite the fact that all the instalments due under the judgment had been paid. The Director General sought an injunction to restrain the use of the standard term on the ground that it was unfair; this application was successful in the Court of Appeal who held that the term was unfair under the previous regulations of 1994; the test of unfairness in those regulations was the same as the current regulations.

That decision was reversed by the House of Lords who held that the clause was not unfair as it did not cause a significant imbalance in the parties' rights and obligations to the detriment of the consumer in a manner contrary to the requirement of good faith. Despite the unpleasant shock that the term might give to consumers, it was legitimate, because without it, the Bank would be unable to charge interest but would not have recovered all of its money until the entire balance on the borrower's account had been repaid.

Figure 1 Applying the Unfair Terms in Consumer Contracts Regulations 1999

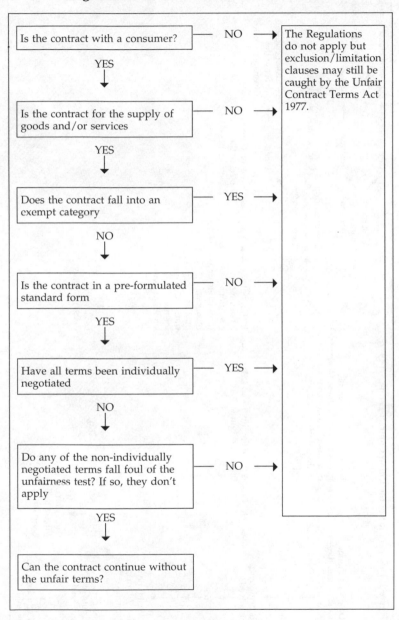

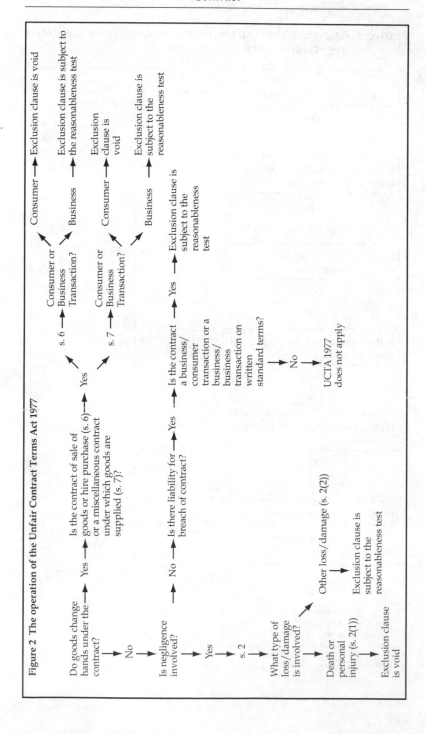

Figure 2 The operation of the Unfair Contract Terms Act 1977

8. MISREPRESENTATION

A statement made during negotiations may, as we have seen, become incorporated into the contract as a term. Alternatively, the statement may form the basis of a collateral contract or it may be a mere representation (see Chapter 6).

If the statement is a contractual term or a collateral contract the remedy for non-compliance is an action for breach of contract. If a mere representation proves false, the remedy will, in most cases, lie in an action for rescission and/or damages for misrepresentation.

An actionable representation renders the contract voidable, i.e. valid until avoided. The definition of actionable misrepresentation, the types of misrepresentation and the remedies available will be considered in this chapter.

ACTIONABLE MISREPRESENTATION

An actionable misrepresentation may be defined as a *false statement of fact* made by one party to the other, which, whilst not being a term of the contract, *induces* the other party to enter the contract. The two elements in italics will now be considered:

False statement of fact

It seems that a statement will be "false" if not "substantially" correct; *Avon Insurance Ltd v Swire Fraser Ltd* (2000).

An actionable misrepresentation is a false statement of some specific existing fact or past event and as a result the following are excluded, i.e. do not amount to misrepresentation if false.

1. Statements of future conduct or intention. A false statement by a person as to what they will do in the future is not misrepresentation; for example, the company prospectus that falsely states that over the next four years, the company will invest a billion pounds. If, however, the statement of intention is a wilful lie, then it may amount to a misrepresentation of fact. In *Edgington v Fitzmaurice*, CA, 1885, company directors raised money from the public by stating that the money would be used to expand the business. In fact, their intention was to use the money to pay off the company's existing debt. The statement was held to be a (fraudulent) misrepresentation of fact.

2. Statements of belief or opinion. A false statement of opinion is not a misrepresentation of fact. In *Bisset v Wilkinson*, PC, 1927, the owner of a farm, which had never before been used as a sheep farm, stated to a prospective purchaser that he believed it would support 2,000 sheep. This was held to be a statement of opinion, not fact.

As with statements of intention (above), if the opinion is not honestly held, there may be a misrepresentation of fact; *Edgington v Fitzmaurice*. Further, if the maker of the statement possesses special knowledge or skill in relation to the subject-matter or is in a stronger position to know the truth, then a statement expressed as an opinion may be held to be an implied misrepresentation of fact; *Smith v Land and House Property Corp*, CA, 1884. "Mere puff" (see Chapter 3) cannot amount to misrepresentation.

3. Statements of law. The traditional rule was that a false statement as to what the law is, could not be actionable misrepresentation. The difficulty of distinguishing between a statement of law and a statement of fact is illustrated by *Solle v Butcher*, CA, 1950, where a statement that a flat was "new" and therefore not subject to the Rent Restriction Acts, was held to be a statement of fact. It would seem that now, however, a misrepresentation of law can constitute actionable misrepresentation; *Pankhania v London Borough of Hackney*, 2002. Statements as to the contents of private Acts of Parliament and as to foreign law are normally regarded as statements of fact.

4. Silence or non-disclosure. The general rule is that to remain silent does not amount to misrepresentation. An example of the rule is *Hands v Simpson Fawcett* (1928). In this case it was held that a commercial traveller who failed to disclose at a job interview that he had had serious motoring convictions made no misrepresentation. He was under no duty, in the circumstances, to disclose them. The rule is a general one and the court is free to conclude that a duty of disclosure arises in particular circumstances; *Sybron Corporation v Rockhem Ltd*, CA, 1983.

The rule is subject to the following exceptions:

(1) Where the statement is a half-truth. A statement that does not present the whole truth may be regarded as a misrepresentation; thus if A, whilst giving credit reference

concerning B, states that B is honest and trustworthy but does not disclose that B has been bankrupt, A may be regarded as making a misrepresentation; *Tapp v Lee* (1803).

(2) Where a statement was true when made but, due to a change of circumstances, has become false by the time it is acted upon. In *With v O'Flanagan*, CA, 1936, the vendor of a medical practice truthfully stated to a prospective purchaser that it was worth £2,000 per annum. The vendor then fell ill, so that, by the time the contract was signed four months later, the receipts had fallen to almost nothing. It was held that the failure of the vendor to disclose this state of affairs to the purchaser amounted to a misrepresentation.

(3) Contracts *uberrimae fidei*, i.e. of the utmost good faith. In this class of contracts, there is a duty to disclose all the material facts as one party is in a strong position to know the truth.

The leading example is contracts of insurance, where there is a duty on the insured to disclose every circumstance which would influence the judgment of the prudent insurer in fixing the premium or deciding whether they will take the risk. Such contracts are voidable.

(4) Parties in a fiduciary relationship. Where such a relationship exists between the parties to a contract, a duty of disclosure will arise, e.g. principal and agent; solicitor and client; partner and partner; doctor and patient.

It is possible to have a misrepresentation purely by conduct. In *Spice Girls v Aprilia World Service BV*, CA, 2002, the defendants agreed to sponsor a Spice Girls tour. The group had appeared in promotional material before the contract was concluded when they knew that one of their number, Geri Halliwell, was about to leave the group. It was held that there had been misrepresentation by conduct.

The meaning of inducement

To amount to a misrepresentation, the false statement must induce the contract. To operate as an inducement, the statement must fulfil the following requirements:

1. The misrepresentation must be addressed to the party misled. In *Peek v Gurney*, HL, 1873, the appellant purchased shares on the faith of a misrepresentation which in fact was intended to mislead a different class of purchaser from that to which the appellant belonged. The House of Lords held that the appellant's action for misrepresentation must fail. However, if it can be shown that the maker of the statement knew that the statement would be passed on to the claimant, then the maker of the statement will be liable in misrepresentation; *Pilmore v Hood* (1838). This principle was applied by the Court of Appeal in *Clef Acquitaine SARL v Laporte Materials (Barrow) Ltd*, CA, 2000.

2. The misrepresentation must be the material inducement. The requirement of materiality is not objective; i.e. whether the misrepresentation would have influenced a reasonable person is of evidentiary value but it is not the determining factor; *Museprime Properties Ltd v Adhill Properties* (1990). However, if the claimant relies on his or her own judgment or investigations, there will be no liability on the part of the misrepresentor. In *Attwood v Small*, HL, 1838, purchasers of a mine were told exaggerated statements as to its earning capacity by the vendors. The purchasers had these statements checked by their own expert agents, who (in error) reported them as correct. It was held that the plaintiffs had been induced to enter the contract by their agents' report and not by the vendors.

If the claimant has a misrepresentation made to him or her and then is offered the means of discovering the truth, but does not take the offer up, the misrepresentation will still be considered as an inducement; *Redgrave v Hurd*, CA, 1881. Further, if the plaintiff is unaware of the misrepresentation at the time of entering the contract, there can be no liability (*Horsfall v Thomas* (1862)), and likewise, though he was aware of it, it is proved that it cannot possibly have affected his judgment; *Smith v Chadwick*, HL, 1884.

To be actionable, the misrepresentation does not have to be the sole factor inducing the claimant to enter the contract; *Edgington v Fitzmaurice*, CA, 1885.

TYPES OF MISREPRESENTATION

In the modern law, misrepresentation is classed as fraudulent, negligent or wholly innocent. These are considered below.

Fraudulent misrepresentation

"Fraudulent" in this sense was defined by Lord Herschell in *Derry v Peek* (1889) as a false statement that is "made (i) knowingly, or (ii) without belief in its truth, or (iii) recklessly, careless as to whether it be true or false". The essence of fraud is absence of honest belief; in *Derry v Peek*, a share prospectus falsely stated that the company had the right to use mechanical power to draw trams, without explaining that governmental consent was required for this. In fact, the directors honestly believed that obtaining consent was a pure formality, although it was ultimately refused. The House of Lords held that there had been no fraudulent misrepresentation.

Negligent misrepresentation

Negligent misrepresentation consists of two types:

1. Negligent misstatement at common law. Until 1963, damages could only be claimed for misrepresentation where it was fraudulent. All non-fraudulent misrepresentations were classed as "innocent" and damages were not available for such innocent misrepresentations. In 1963, the House of Lords stated, *obiter*, in *Hedley Byrne Co Ltd v Heller Partners Ltd*, HL, 1964, that in certain circumstances damages may be recoverable in tort for negligent misstatement causing financial loss. The liability depends on a duty of care arising from a "special relationship" between the parties. It is now clear that a party can claim damages under the principle in Hedley Byrne where a negligent misstatement has induced him or her to enter a contract; *Esso Petroleum Co Ltd v Mardon*, CA, 1976. Broadly speaking, the special relationship will only arise where the maker of the statement possesses knowledge or skill relevant to the subject-matter of the contract and can reasonably foresee that the other party will rely on the statement.

2. Negligent misrepresentation under the Misrepresentation Act 1967. Section 2(1) of the Act of 1967 introduced, for the first time, a statutory claim for damages for non-fraudulent misrepresentation. Section 2(1) provides that where a person has entered a contract after a misrepresentation has been made to them by another party thereto, and, as a result thereof, they have suffered loss, then, if the person making the misrepresentation would be liable to damages in respect thereof had the misrepresentation been made fraudulently, that person shall be so liable notwithstanding that the misrepresentation was not made fraudulently, unless they prove that they had reasonable ground to believe and did believe, up to the time the contract was made, that the facts represented were true.

It should be noted that the sub-section assumes all non fraudulent statements to be negligent and puts the burden on the maker of the statement to disprove negligence.

Wholly innocent misrepresentation

We have seen that, before 1963, the word "innocent" was used to describe all misrepresentations that were not fraudulent. In the light of *Hedley Byrne* and s.2(1) of the Act of 1967, the word innocent may now be used to refer to a statement made by a person who has reasonable grounds for believing in its truth. To avoid confusion, "wholly innocent" is a better description.

REMEDIES FOR MISREPRESENTATION

Once an actionable misrepresentation is established, it becomes necessary to consider the remedies available to the misrepresentee. The remedies are as follows.

Rescission

Rescission, i.e. setting aside the contract, is possible whether the misrepresentation is fraudulent, negligent or innocent.

Where a contract is rescinded it is terminated *ab initio*; the object is to put the parties back in the position they would have been in had the contract never been made. The injured party may elect to rescind the contract. This can be done by notifying the other party or by any other act indicating repudiation of liability, e.g. notifying the authorities; *Car and Universal Finance Co Ltd v Caldwell*, CA, 1964. The injured party may also apply to the court for an order of rescission. An order of rescission may be accompanied by the court ordering an indemnity. This is a money payment by the misrepresentor to restore the parties to their position as if the contract had never been made. An indemnity is payable in respect of obligations necessarily created by the contract and it should be distinguished from damages. The distinction is illustrated by *Whittington v Seale-Hayne* (1900). The claimants bred poultry and took a lease of the defendant's premises, as a result of an innocent misrepresentation that the premises were sanitary. In fact, the water supply was poisoned and the defendants submitted to rescission. The claimants requested an indemnity to cover: (i) loss of profits; (ii) value of stock lost; (iii) removal costs; (iv) medical expenses; (v) rent and rates; and (vi) the cost of repairs ordered by the local council. It was held that an indemnity would be awarded in respect of items (v) and (vi) only, as these were obligations necessarily created by the contract. As the claimants were not obliged to carry on a business, items (i)–(iv), had they been awarded, would have amounted to an award of damages.

The power to award an indemnity is not affected by the Misrepresentation Act 1967, although it will not be applicable where damages are in fact awarded. Thus, the remedy remains particularly significant where the contract is rescinded for a wholly innocent misrepresentation.

Bars to rescission

The injured party may lose the right to rescind in the following circumstances ("bars to rescission").

1. Affirmation. The injured party will affirm the contract if, with full knowledge of the misrepresentation and of his right to rescind, they expressly state that they intend to continue with it, or if they do an act from which the intention may be implied; *Long v Lloyd*, CA, 1958; *Peyman v Lanjani*, CA, 1985.

Lapse of time may be evidence of affirmation, although where the misrepresentation is fraudulent, the time which is evidence of affirmation runs from the time when the fraud was, or with reasonable diligence could have been discovered. There is authority that in the case of non-fraudulent misrepresentation, time runs from the date of the contract, not the date of discovery of the misrepresentation; *Leaf v International Galleries*, CA, 1950.

2. Impossibility of restitution. The injured party will lose the right to rescind if the parties cannot be restored to their original position. In *Vigers v Pike* (1842), a lease of a mine which had been entered into as a result of a misrepresentation could not be rescinded as there had been considerable extraction of minerals since the date of the contract. It should be noted that precise restoration is not required and the remedy is still available if substantial restoration is possible.

Deterioration in the value or condition of property is not a bar; *Armstrong v Jackson* (1917).

3. Third party rights. Rescission cannot be ordered where third party rights have accrued, bona fide and for value.

Thus, if A obtains goods from B by misrepresentation and sells them to C, who takes in good faith, B cannot later rescind on learning of the misrepresentation in order to recover the goods from C; *White v Garden* (1851).

Two further bars to rescission were abolished by s.1 of the Misrepresentation Act 1967, namely where the misrepresentation had become incorporated as a contractual term and where, after a non-fraudulent misrepresentation, the contract had been executed.

Damages for misrepresentation

Damages for misrepresentation may be claimed or awarded under the following heads.

1. Damages for fraudulent misrepresentation. The claim for such damages is a claim in the tort of deceit. The object is to restore the claimant to the position they would have been in had the representation not been made, i.e. the amount by which the plaintiff is out of pocket by entering the contract; *McConnel v Wright*, CA, 1903. The "out of pocket" rule does not necessarily preclude a claim for loss of profits as illustrated by *East v Maurer*, CA, 1991 in which the claimant purchased a hairdressing salon on the basis of a fraudulent misrepresentation. Damages were awarded for the profit the claimant might have made had he bought a different salon in the same area, i.e. he could recover for the "opportunity cost" of relying on the misrepresentation. However, the basis of damages for breach of contract is normally the loss of bargain basis, (see Chapter 14).

It seems that the test of remoteness in deceit is that the claimant may recover for all the direct loss incurred as a result of the fraudulent inducement, regardless of foreseeability; *Doyle v Olby (Ironmongers) Ltd*, CA, 1969, affirmed by the House of Lords in *Smith New Court Securities Ltd v Scrimgeour Vickers (Asset Management) Ltd*, HL, 1996. Although the law is unclear as to whether exemplary damages may be awarded, aggravated damages may be awarded in deceit to compensate the claimant for distress: *Archer v Brown* (1985).

In *Downs v Chappell*, CA, 1977, it was held that the misrepresentee is under a duty to mitigate his or her loss once the fraudulent misrepresentation has been discovered, i.e. the claimant must take reasonable steps to minimise the loss.

2. Damages for negligent misrepresentation. The claimant may elect to claim damages under the principle in

Hedley Byrne v Heller providing the ingredients of the tort are established. The award of damages under *Hedley Byrne* differs from damages in deceit only in that, under *Hedley Byrne*, the remoteness test is that of reasonable foreseeability.

Alternatively the claimant may claim damages for negligent misrepresentation under s.2(1) of the Act of 1967 and where the claimant has entered a contract as a result of the misrepresentation this will be the normal course to pursue, as opposed to an action in tort. Under s.2(1) the maker of the statement is deemed negligent and bears the burden of disproving negligence. This is the most significant advantage of a claim under s.2(1) over *Hedley Byrne*.

The fact that the maker of the statement bears a heavy burden of proof under s.2(1) is illustrated by *Howard Marine and Dredging Co Ltd v A. Ogden and Sons (Excavations) Ltd*, CA, 1978. Here, in negotiations to hire out two sea-going barges, the owners' representative misrepresented the carrying capacity of the barges. He relied on Lloyds Register which was in fact incorrect; the correct information was on file at the owners' head office. The Court of Appeal held that there was liability under s.2(1); the presumption of negligence had not been disproved. Where a misrepresentation is made by an agent of the contracting party, the injured party can only bring an action under s.2(1) against the contracting party and not the agent; *Resolute Maritime v Nippon Kaiji Kyokai* (1983).

Royscot Trust Ltd v Rogerson, CA, 1991 established that damages under s.2(1) are to be assessed on the same basis as fraudulent misrepresentation, although doubts were expressed as to this in the *Smith New Court Securities Case* (above). Indeed, this so-called "fiction of fraud" under s.2(1) has caused some controversy, since the remoteness rule for fraud (discussed above), can produce a very high level of damages for what is essentially negligence, not fraud. This was acknowledged by Rix J. in *Avon Insurance Ltd v Swire Fraser Ltd* (2000) where he said the courts should not be too willing to find a negligent misrepresentation where there was room for the exercise of judgment. In *Gran Gelato v Richcliff (Group) Ltd* (1992) it was held that damages awarded under s.2(1) could be reduced by reason of the contributory negligience of the plaintiff, however this has no application to actions in fraud; *Alliance and Leicester Building Society v Edgestop Ltd* (1994).

3. Damages in lieu of rescission. It is clear that damages may not be claimed for a wholly innocent misrepresentation, i.e. one that is neither fraudulent or negligent. The only remedy for wholly innocent misrepresentation is rescission, which may be accompanied by an indemnity.

The previous paragraph is subject to the following. Section 2(2) of the Misrepresentation Act 1967 gives the court a discretion, where the injured party would be entitled to rescind, to award damages in lieu of rescission. Damages under s.2(2) cannot be claimed as such; they can only be awarded by the court. The power of the court under the sub-section can only be used in the case of non-fraudulent (i.e. negligent and wholly innocent) misrepresentation. It had always been assumed that the loss of the right to rescind (e.g. by affirmation) would remove this power to award damages, however this was not accepted in *Thomas Witter Ltd v TBP Industries* (1996). Further, the measure of damages under s.2(2) was considered in *William Sindall Plc v Cambridgeshire County Council*, CA, 1994 where Evans L.J. suggested that it should be "the difference in value between what the [claimant] was misled into believing he was acquiring, and the value of what he in fact received." Where damages are awarded under s.2(1), the court must (by virtue of s.2(3)) take into account any damages awarded in lieu of rescission under s.2(2).

EXCLUSION OF LIABILITY FOR MISREPRESENTATION

Section 3 of the Misrepresentation Act 1967, as amended by s.8 of the Unfair Contract Terms Act 1977, provides that if a contract contains a term which would exclude or restrict:

(1) any liability to which a party to a contract may be subject by reason of any misrepresentation made by him or her before the contract was made; or

(2) any remedy available to another party to the contract by reason of such a misrepresentation, that term shall be of no effect except in so far as it satisfies the requirement of reasonableness as stated in s.11(1) of the Unfair Contract Terms Act 1977 (see Chapter 6); and it is for those claiming that the term satisfies that requirement to show that it does.

Section 3 cannot be evaded by the contract term in question deeming that statements of fact are not representations; *Cremdean Properties Ltd v Nash* (1977). However, a term which stated that an auctioneer had no authority to make any representation was held to fall outside s.3; *Overbrooke Estates Ltd v Glencombe Properties Ltd* (1974).

An entire agreement clause (see Chapter 6) does not preclude a claim in misrepresentation. Insofar as such a clause seeks to do so, it may fall under s.3.

Further, s.3 does not invalidate a contractual provision that the contract contains the entire terms of the contract; *McGrath v Shah* (1989).

Figure 3: Action guide to misrepresentation

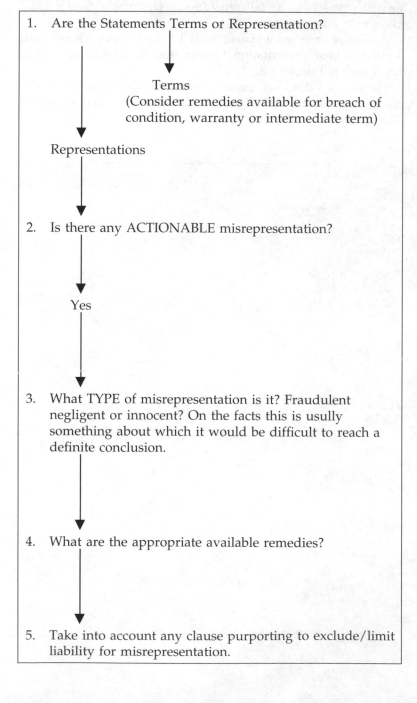

1. Are the Statements Terms or Representation?

   Terms
   (Consider remedies available for breach of
   condition, warranty or intermediate term)

   Representations

2. Is there any ACTIONABLE misrepresentation?

   Yes

3. What TYPE of misrepresentation is it? Fraudulent
   negligent or innocent? On the facts this is usully
   something about which it would be difficult to reach a
   definite conclusion.

4. What are the appropriate available remedies?

5. Take into account any clause purporting to exclude/limit
   liability for misrepresentation.

9. MISTAKE

In certain circumstances, a contract may be void at common law owing to a mistake made by the parties concerning the contract. The situations in which a contract will be nullified for mistake are contained in a disparate group of cases; there is no underlying general "doctrine" of mistake. A mistake which has the effect of rendering a contract void is described as an "operative" mistake. However, in determining the issue of mistake, whether at common law or in equity, there is a threshold question that first has to be considered, i.e. whether the contract itself, expressly or impliedly, provides which party should bear the risk of the mistake; *Kalsep Ltd v X-Flow BV* (2001).

The scope of operative mistake now extends to mistakes of law as well as fact; *Kleinwort Benson Ltd v Lincoln City Council*, HL, 1999 and *Brennan v Bolt Burden*, CA, 2004. The law relating to mistake will be considered under four heads: Mistake relating to documents; Identical or "common" mistake; Non-identical mistake; Mistake as to identity.

MISTAKE RELATING TO DOCUMENTS

Non est factum

As a general rule, a person is bound by his or her signature to a document, whether or not they have read or understood the document; *L'Estrange v Graucob* (1934). Where a person has been induced to sign a contractual document by fraud or misrepresentation, the transaction will be voidable. Similarly, if one of the other forms of mistake discussed in this chapter are present the contract may be void.

In the absence of these factors, the plea of *non est factum* (not my deed) may be available. The plea is an ancient one and was originally used to protect illiterate persons. It eventually became available to literate persons who had signed a document believing it to be something totally different from what it actually was. Thus, in *Foster v Mackinnon* (1869), the defendant, a senile man with poor eyesight, was induced to sign a document which he was told was a guarantee. In fact, it was a bill of exchange upon which the claimant ultimately became entitled. It was held that the defendant, who had not been negligent, was not liable on the bill; the plea of *non est factum* succeeded.

An unrestrained right to raise the plea would lead to abuse and uncertainty and so the courts have placed two restrictions on the right to raise the plea, (i) the signer's mistake as to the nature of the document must be fundamental or radical; and (ii) the signer must not have been careless in signing the document.

With regard to (i), the courts originally took the view that the plea was not available where the signer's mistake was merely as to the contents of the document rather than as to its character or class; *Howatson v Webb*, CA, 1908. This test was not a realistic one and was substituted by the *House of Lords in Saunders v Anglia Building Society*, HL, 1971. The test is now that there must be a fundamental or radical difference between the document actually signed and what the signer believed it to be.

With regard to (ii), the Court of Appeal had ruled in *Carlisle and Cumberland Banking Co v Bragg*, CA, 1911 that negligence on the part of the signer only defeated the plea if the document was a negotiable instrument. The distinction was illogical and *Bragg's case* was overruled by *Saunders*; the position is now that the plea cannot be raised by a signer who has been careless.

In *Saunders v Anglia Building Society*, an elderly widow wished to transfer the title of her house to her nephew by way of gift. Her nephew and a man named Lee prepared a document assigning the property to Lee and asked her to sign. She signed it unread as she had lost her spectacles and trusted her nephew. Lee mortgaged the property to the Building Society and disposed of the moneys raised for his own use. He defaulted on the repayments and the Building Society sought possession of the house. Saunders (the widow's executrix) sought a declaration that the assignment to Lee was void by reason of *non est factum*.

In the view of both the Court of Appeal and the House of Lords, the plea could not be raised because, (i) the transaction the widow had entered was not fundamentally different from what she intended at the time she entered it; and (ii) she had been careless in signing the document; she could at least have made sure that the transfer was to the person intended by her. The effect of *Saunders v Anglia Building Society* is, if anything, to restrict further the circumstances in which the plea of *non est factum* can be successfully raised.

Rectification

Where the parties are agreed on the terms of the contract but by mistake record them incorrectly in a subsequent written document, the remedy of rectification may be available. The court can rectify the error and order specific performance of the contract as rectified.

The remedy is an exception to the parol evidence rule (see Chapter 6) as oral evidence is admissible to show that the written document is in error.

In order to obtain rectification the following must be established:

(1) There must be a concluded antecedent agreement upon which the written document was based. The agreement need not necessarily be a finally binding contract; *Josceleyne v Nissen* (1970).

(2) The written document must fail to record what the parties had agreed. In *Frederick E. Rose (London) Ltd v William H. Pim Co Ltd*, CA, 1953, the parties had contracted for the sale of a type of horsebean and the written contract referred to "horsebeans". The goods delivered were not of the type the parties had in mind. Rectification was refused since the written contract correctly recorded what the parties had agreed.

(3) The written document must fail to express the common intention of the parties. However, if one party mistakenly believes the document gives effect to that intention and the other party is aware of this mistake but nevertheless is guilty of sharp practice in allowing the contract to be executed, rectification may be ordered; *A. Roberts Co v Leicestershire C.C.* (1961).

(4) It must be equitable to grant the remedy; in particular, it will be refused where third parties have acquired rights on the faith of the written contract.

IDENTICAL OR COMMON MISTAKE

Here, the parties, although apparently in agreement, have entered into a contract on the basis of a false and fundamental assumption. It may be described as identical or common mistake since both parties make the same error. The contract is not necessarily void at common law in these circumstances. The cases may be categorised as follows.

Mistake as to the existence of the subject-matter

The contract will be void at common law if, unknown to the parties, the subject-matter of the agreement does not exist or has ceased to exist. In *Couturier v Hastie*, HL, 1856, a cargo of corn, en route to London, had to be sold at a port of refuge as it had begun to ferment. Unaware of this, the parties agreed a sale of the corn in London. It was held that the seller was not entitled to the price of the cargo.

Similarly, the parties may contract on the basis of a false assumption which underlies the contract. In *Galloway v Galloway* (1914), a man and woman, believing they were lawfully married, entered into a separation deed. In fact the "marriage" was invalid and therefore the separation agreement was likewise void.

It may be, however, that the proper construction of the contract is that the risk of the subject-matter or state of affairs not being in existence falls on one party or the other. For example, one party may be warranting the existence of the subject-matter; if so, the contract is valid; *McRae v Commonwealth Disposals Commission* (1950).

In *Great Peace Shipping Ltd v Tsavliris (Salvage) International Ltd* (2001) the ship Great Providence was damaged and in danger of sinking. The owners engaged the defendants to recover her, and the defendants were informed by a third party that the claimants' ship Great Peace was in close proximity. The defendants accordingly hired the Great Peace for a minimum of five days to assist in her recovery. The claimants sought to recover the hire. Toulson J. held that the contract was not void at common law as the mistake was not sufficiently fundamental; the Great Peace was not so far away as to be incapable of providing the service required. Thus, the risk fell on the defendants. This decision was subsequently affirmed by the Court of Appeal.

Mistake as to title

The contract will be void at common law in the (rare) situation where one party agrees to transfer property to the other which the latter already owns and neither party is aware of the fact. In *Cooper v Phibbs*, HL, 1867, the House of Lords set aside an agreement whereby A had agreed to lease a fishery to B, but unknown to either, the fishery was already owned by B.

Mistake as to quality

There is authority that an identical mistake as to the quality of the subject-matter is not operative at common law. Thus, if A sells to B a painting which both parties mistakenly believe to have been painted by Constable, and therefore valuable, but in fact which is not by Constable and is worth far less, the contract is valid (in the absence of actionable misrepresentation or assumption of risk by either party); *Leaf v International Galleries*, CA, 1950.

The leading case is *Bell v Lever Bros Ltd*, HL, 1932. Bell, an employee of Lever, entered into an agreement to terminate his employment under which he was paid £30,000 compensation. It was later discovered that Bell could have been dismissed without compensation due to certain breaches of contract by him and about which he had forgotten. The House of Lords was prepared to treat the case as a common mistake as to quality, but held the contract valid.

As the mistake in *Bell v Lever Bros* was surely fundamental, the case has been interpreted as deciding that an identical mistake as to quality can never render the contract void at common law. Subsequent decisions tend to support this view, for example, *Leaf v International Galleries* and *Harrison and Jones Ltd v Bunten and Lancaster Ltd* (1953), where there was a sale of Kapok identified as "Sree Brand". Both parties mistakenly believed that Sree was pure Kapok when it was not. The contract was held valid. Nevertheless, there are dicta in the speeches of the House of Lords in *Bell v Lever Bros* which suggest that a contract may be void if the mistake as to quality is sufficiently fundamental, and support for this view is to be found in the cases of *Associated Japanese Bank Ltd v Credit du Nord* (1988) and *Great Peace (Shipping) Ltd v Tsavliris (Salvage) International Ltd*, CA, 2002.

Identical or common mistake in equity

Until quite recently, it was accepted that where there was a common mistake as to quality, although the agreement was valid at law, it was apparently voidable in equity. Thus, in *Solle v Butcher*, CA, 1950, the claimant agreed to lease a flat from the defendant, both parties mistakenly believing that the premises were not subject to rent-control. The Court of Appeal held that the mistake was not such as would render the lease void at law, but the court would set aside the contract in equity. To do justice, terms were imposed that the claimant should either give up the flat or stay on at the maximum rent chargeable by law.

Similar examples of rescission in equity of contracts entered into under an identical mistake as to quality were *Grist v Bailey*

(1967) (sale of a house) and *Magee v Pennine Insurance Co Ltd*, CA, 1969 (contract of insurance) However, these authorities require re-appraisal as a result of the *Great Peace Shipping* case (discussed above) where Toulson J. controversially doubted the very existence of the doctrine of rescission in equity of a contract on the grounds of common mistake. The judge was "at a loss as to what is the test for determining the nature of the 'fundamental mistake' necessary to give birth to the right to rescind". This approach was affirmed by the Court of Appeal who held that there is no jurisdiction to grant rescission of a contract on the ground of common mistake where that contract is valid and enforceable on common law grounds. Thus, the court disapproved *Solle v Butcher* on the basis that it was not good law.

NON-IDENTICAL MISTAKE

In this type of case, the parties do not both make the same mistake. A non-identical mistake is said to be "mutual" where the parties misunderstand each other's intentions and are at cross-purposes, and "unilateral" where only one party is mistaken and the other party is aware of the mistake.

Mutual mistake

Operative mutual mistake is illustrated by *Raffles v Wichelhaus* (1864). The defendants agreed to buy cotton from the claimants ex the ship "Peerless" from Bombay. Two ships of that name were due to leave Bombay; the defendants had in mind the ship leaving in October and the claimants had in mind the ship leaving in December. The court held that the transaction was too ambiguous to be enforced as a contract.

The test applied by the court in this type of case is to consider whether a reasonable third party would take the agreement to mean what one party, A, understood it to mean or what the other party, B, understood it to mean. It is only when the transaction is totally ambiguous under this objective test that the contract is void. Thus, in *Wood v Scarth* (1858) the defendant offered in writing to let a pub to the claimant at £63 per annum. After a conversation with the defendant's clerk, the claimant accepted by letter, believing that the £63 rental was the only payment under the contract. The defendant had intended that a £500 premium would also be payable and he believed that his clerk had explained this to the claimant. It was held that the contract as understood by the claimant would be enforced and the court awarded him damages.

By comparison, in *Scriven v Hindley* (1913), at an auction, the defendants' bid for a lot consisting of tow was accepted. The defendants believed that they had bid for hemp. Their bid was right for hemp but extravagant for tow, although the auctioneer was unaware of the true nature of the defendants' mistake. However, the catalogue and samples were misleadingly described and marked, and these factors, together with other circumstances, meant that the reasonable person could not say whether the contract was for hemp or tow. The contract was held to be void.

Mutual mistake in equity

If the contract is void at law on the ground of a mutual mistake, equity "follows the law" and an order of specific performance will be refused. However, even where the contract is valid at law, specific performance will be refused if to grant it would cause hardship. Thus, the remedy of specific performance was refused in *Wood v Scarth* (see above).

Unilateral mistake

Here one party is fundamentally mistaken concerning the contract and the other party is aware of the mistake, or the circumstances are such that he may be taken to be aware of it.

For a unilateral mistake to be operative, the mistake by one party must be as to the terms of the contract itself, as in *Hartog v Colin and Shields* (1939). Here the defendants offered goods to the claimant at a certain price per pound but had intended to offer them at the same price per piece. The value of a piece was one third that of a pound. It was held that the circumstances were such that the claimants must have realised the defendant's error, which, as it concerned a term of the contract, rendered the contract void.

A mere error of judgment as to the quality of the subject-matter will not suffice to render the contract void for unilateral mistake. In *Smith v Hughes* (1871), the defendant was shown a sample of new oats by the claimant. The defendant bought them in the belief that they were "old" oats; he did not want "new" oats. The court was of the view that the mistake was merely as to quality of the subject-matter and could not render the contract void, even if the claimant seller knew of the mistake.

Unilateral mistake in equity

As with mutual mistake, equity follows the law and will refuse specific performance of a contract affected by unilateral mistake as in _Webster v Cecil_ (1861). In that case, the defendant, who had already refused to sell his property to the plaintiff for £2,000, wrote offering to sell it to him for £1,250. This offer was immediately accepted. The defendant had intended to write £2,250. It was held that the mistake was operative and specific performance would be refused.

MISTAKE AS TO IDENTITY

Where one party is mistaken as to the identity of the other party, in certain circumstances the contract may be void at common law.

Almost all the decided cases of operative mistake in this area are in fact instances of unilateral mistake, as the non-mistaken party is aware of the mistake because they have engineered it through their own fraud. Even where the contract is not void, it may be voidable for fraudulent misrepresentation and if the goods which are the subject-matter have passed to an innocent third party before the contract is avoided, that third party may acquire a good title (see below for examples).

For the contract to be void, certain requirements must be satisfied.

1. The identity of the other party must be of crucial importance. In _Cundy v Lindsay_, HL, 1878, the claimants received an order for linen from a rogue, Blenkarn, who gave his address as 37 Wood Street, Cheapside. In the correspondence, he imitated the signature of a reputable firm, Blenkiron and Co, known to the claimants, who traded at 123 Wood Street, Cheapside. The claimants were thus fraudulently induced to send goods to Blenkarn's address, where he took possession of them and disposed of them to the defendants, innocent purchasers. It was held that the contract between the claimants and Blenkarn was void for mistake as the claimants intended to deal only with Blenkiron and Co. No title in the goods passed to Blenkarn (because the contract was void) and therefore none passed to the defendants who were liable in conversion to the claimants.

Identity was held not to be crucial in _Phillips v Brooks_ (1919). Here, a rogue called North entered the claimant's shop and, having selected some jewellery, wrote a cheque and announced himself as Sir George Bullough of St. James' Square, a man of means of whom the claimant had heard. The claimant, having checked this address in a directory, allowed North to take away a ring. North then pledged the ring with the defendants, who had no notice of the fraud. In an action by the claimant's to recover the ring from the defendants, it was held that the contract between the claimant's and North was not void for mistake, because the claimants had intended to contract with the person in the shop, whoever it was. The only mistake was as to the customer's credit-worthiness, not his identity. The contract was, however, voidable for fraud but because the defendants had acquired the ring in good faith before the contract was sought to be set aside, they acquired a good title.

Despite *Phillips v Brooks*, identity was held to be crucial in *Ingram v Little*, CA, 1961. The claimants, elderly ladies, advertised their car for sale. A rogue, calling himself P. G. M. Hutchinson of an address in Caterham, offered to buy it. The claimants would only accept a cheque when they had checked, from a directory, that there was such a person at that address. The cheque was worthless and the rogue disposed of the car to the defendant, who took in good faith. It was held that the contract between the claimants and the rogue was void for mistake. The decision in this case is very difficult to distinguish from *Phillips v Brooks*.

The decision in *Phillips v Brooks* was followed by Court of Appeal in *Lewis v Averay*, CA, 1972, where the claimant, a postgraduate student, advertised a car for sale and was visited by a rogue posing as the actor Richard Greene, who offered to buy it. The rogue signed a cheque but the claimant only allowed him to take the car away after being shown a forged studio admission pass. The cheque was worthless and the rogue sold the car to the defendant, an innocent purchaser. The Court of Appeal held that the contract, though voidable, was not void. The court took the view that, where the parties are face to face, there is a presumption that a person intends to deal with the person before him, as identified by sight and hearing. There was insufficient evidence in this case that the claimant intended to deal only with the well-known actor.

A mistake as to identity should be distinguished from a mistake as to the capacity in which a party deals. Thus, in *Hardman v Booth* (1863), the claimants, intending to sell cloth to Thomas Glandell Co, negotiated with one Edward Gandell at the firm's offices. Edward, an employee and not a member of the firm, intended to take possession of the goods for his own use. Having obtained possession, he sold them to the defendant, an innocent third party. It was held that the contract between the claimants and Edward was void. The claimants had believed he was a representative of the firm and never intended to deal with him personally.

It is sometimes stated that an additional requirement for the contract to be void is that the mistaken party must have taken reasonable steps to verify the identity of the other party. It may be that this is more in the nature of an evidential burden to establish that the identity of the other party is crucial. The issue of mistaken identity arose in *Shogun Finance Ltd v Norman Hudson*, HL, 2002, where a rogue X went to a dealer to buy a car on hire purchase. X produced the stolen driving licence of P and the dealer checked these details with the claimant finance company, which approved the transaction. X then sold the vehicle to an innocent purchaser. The claimant finance company argued that the agreement with X was void because they intended only to contract with P and the identity of P was a matter of vital importance. The Court of Appeal held that H did not obtain a good title; i.e. the hire purchase contract was void, and a majority of the House of Lords affirmed this decision. The finance company was only willing to do business with the person identified in the written agreement and no one else. Thus, the face to face principle has no application to a case where the contract is wholly in writing. In such cases the identity of the vendor and purchaser is established by the names of the parties included in the written contract.

In arriving at this decision, their Lordships held that H had not acquired good title under s.27 Hire Purchase Act 1964. Under that provision, a private purchaser, acting in good faith without notice of the hire purchase agreement, who buys a car from a seller (a "debtor") who in turn holds the car under a hire purchase agreement, will obtain a good title. However, it was held that the debtor under the hire purchase agreement was P, not the rogue, and so the 1964 act did not apply.

2. The mistaken party must have in mind an identifiable person with whom they intend to contract. This requirement was not satisfied in *King's Norton Metal Co v Edridge Merrett Co Ltd*, CA, 1897. The claimants received a letter purporting to be from "Hallam & Co" with an impressive letterhead. In fact

Hallam was a fictitious firm consisting entirely of a rogue named Wallis. The claimants despatched goods on credit to the bogus company. The court took the view that the claimants had intended to contract with the writer of the letter, whoever it may be, and the contract was not void for mistake. The only mistake was as to the credit-worthiness of the other party and not as to his identity. This decision should be compared with *Cundy v Lindsay* (above).

3. The other party must be aware of the mistake. In the cases discussed above, identity was fraudulently misrepresented and therefore the requirement was satisfied. An unusual case in this context is *Boulton v Jones* (1857). The claimant was employed by Brocklehurst, a pipe hose manufacturer, with whom the defendants had had previous dealings. The claimant took over Brocklehurst's business and on the same day the defendants ordered hose from Brocklehurst. The claimant supplied the goods but the defendants refused to pay on the ground that they intended to contract, not with the claimant, but with Brocklehurst as they wished to enforce a set-off against him. It was held that there was no contract, although the precise state of knowledge of the claimant was not made clear. If the claimant was unaware of the fact that the offer was not intended for him then, arguably, the contract was valid.

10. DURESS AND UNDUE INFLUENCE

The agreement may be the result of some improper pressure exerted by one party over the other. The problem is dealt with by the common law doctrine of duress and the equitable doctrine of undue influence.

DURESS

Duress is a common law concept under which a contract may be avoided. It seems that duress renders a contract voidable; *Pao On v Lau Yiu Long*, PC, 1980.

The scope of duress at common law was very narrow and confined to unlawful physical violence to the person or constraint of the other party (actual or threatened); *Cumming v Ince* (1847). In particular, the courts refused to recognise "duress of goods" as invalidating a contract. However, modern cases indicate a more flexible approach; in *The Siboen and the Sibotre* (1976) it was said that a person coerced into a contract by the threat of having his house burnt down or a picture slashed could plead duress. It seems that "coercion of the will" is now the essence of duress. In *Pao On* Lord Scarman said that in determining whether there was a coercion of the will such that there was no consent, it is material whether the person alleged to have been coerced did or did not protest, whether at the time they did or did not have an alternative course open to them, such as an adequate legal remedy, whether they were independently advised and whether, after entering the contract, they took steps to avoid it.

Based on *Pao On* and other cases the courts are presently evolving a doctrine of "economic duress". For example, in *North Ocean Shipping Co Ltd v Hyundai Construction Co Ltd* (1978), a contract was made to build a supertanker for an agreed price. The seller then refused to complete unless the buyer promised to pay a further ten per cent. The buyer agreed and made the payments as the ship was needed to fulfil a charter. It was held that the extra payment could in principle be recovered on the ground of economic duress although on the facts of the case it was held that the buyer had affirmed the contract because he had complained too late. However, in the more recent case of *Atlas Express Ltd v Kafco* (1989) (where economic duress was found) it was said that duress requires coercion of the will so as to vitiate consent and that "mere commercial pressure" is not sufficient. The dividing line between the two will always be difficult to draw and may depend upon a close examination of the facts of the particular case, however in *CTN Cash and Carry v Gallagher*, CA, 1994 it was suggested that, in appropriate circumstances, a threat to commit a lawful act could amount to duress. This represents a potentially difficult extension of the doctrine. The most recent definition of economic duress was provided by Dyson J. in *DSND Subsea Ltd v Petroleum Geo-Services ASA* (2000) where he said:

> "The ingredients of actionable duress are that there must be pressure, (a) whose practical effect is that there is compulsion on, or a lack of practical choice for, the victim; (b) which is illegitimate; and (c) which is a significant cause inducing the claimant to enter into the contract. In determining whether there has been illegitimate pressure, the court takes into account a range of factors. These include whether there has been an actual or threatened breach of contract; whether the person allegedly exerting the pressure has acted in good or bad faith; whether the victim had any realistic alternative but to submit to the pressure; whether the victim protested at the time; and whether he affirmed and sought to rely on the contract . . . [i]llegitimate pressure must be distinguished from the rough and tumble of the pressures of normal commercial bargaining."

To avoid a contract on the ground of duress, the duress need not be the only or main reason for entering the contract; *Barton v Armstrong*, PC, 1975.

UNDUE INFLUENCE

The narrow scope of the common law doctrine of duress led to the development, in equity, of the doctrine of undue influence. Historically, the doctrine applied wherever improper pressure (not amounting to duress at common law) was brought to bear on a party to enter a contract.

The cases fall into two categories:

(1) No special fiduciary relationship: Where no such relationship exists, the person pressed into the contract must prove that undue influence was applied. For example, in *Williams v Bayley* (HL, 1866) it was established that a promise to pay money will be set aside if obtained by a threat to prosecute the promisor or his spouse or close relative for a criminal offence. In *CIBC Mortgages Plc v*

Pitt, HL, 1993 it was held that the transaction does not have to be to the victim's manifest disadvantage before the court will exercise its power to rescind.

(2) Where a special fiduciary relationship exists: A transaction may be set aside on the ground that a presumption of undue influence arises from the nature of the relationship between the parties. The dominant party must prove that no undue influence has been exercised; it is irrelevant that the dominant party obtained no personal benefit.

The presumption applies to the following relationships: parent and child, guardian and ward, religious advisor and disciple, solicitor and client, trustee and beneficiary. It does not apply between husband and wife. The presumption, where it applies, may continue for a short time after the relationship has ceased. It is sufficient, in such cases, for the claimant to establish the existence of such a relationship and that the transaction calls for an explanation; *Royal Bank of Scotland Plc v Etridge (No 2)*, HL, 2001.

An inference of undue influence may also apply even if the relationship is not within one of the above relationships but one party, by reason of the confidence reposed in him or her by the other weaker party, is able to take unfair advantage. For example, in *Lloyds Bank Ltd v Bundy*, CA, 1975, an elderly farmer gave the Bank a guarantee in respect of his son's overdraft and mortgaged the farmhouse to the Bank as security. It was clear that the farmer had placed himself entirely in the hands of the assistant bank manager and had been given no opportunity to seek independent advice. Although, normally, the presumption of undue influence would not apply between bank and customer, the Court of Appeal held that it did so here and the transaction was set aside.

It was later held by the House of Lords in *National Westminster Bank Plc v Morgan*, HL, 1985 that the transaction would only be avoided in cases of presumed undue influence where the transaction itself was "manifestly disadvantageous" to the weaker party. However, in *Royal Bank of Scotland Plc v Etridge (No 2)*, HL, 2000 their Lordships considered that the label "manifest disadvantage" should be abandoned in favour of a test of whether the transaction "calls for an explanation", thus adopting the dictum of Lindley J. in *Allcard v Skinner*, 1887: i.e. is the transaction such as "not to be reasonably accounted for on the ground of friendship, relationship, charity or other ordinary motives on which ordinary men act?"

In *Lloyds Bank v Bundy*, Lord Denning M.R. had sought to establish a doctrine whereby all the instances where the courts intervene to set aside unconscionable transactions are based on a single unifying principle, namely, "inequality of bargaining power". In *National Westminster Bank v Morgan*, the House of Lords refused to accept such a wide principle. Lord Scarman said, ". . . there is no precisely defined law setting limits to the equitable jurisdiction of a court to relieve against undue influence".

The presumption of undue influence may be rebutted by the beneficiary of the transaction showing that the other party exercised independent free will. This is normally done by proving that the other party received competent independent advice.

UNDUE INFLUENCE AND THIRD PARTIES

In *Barclays Bank Plc v O'Brien*, HL, 1993 the House of Lords sought to lay down authoritative guidance on the question of undue influence, misrepresentation or other legal wrong exercised by a third party. Their Lordships based their approach on the doctrine of notice. The facts of the case were that a husband misrepresented to his wife the amount of a loan sought from the creditor bank. The wife guaranteed the loan. The transaction was set aside, the House of Lords holding that the bank, being aware that the parties were husband and wife, was put on notice of the possibility of legal wrong. However, the bank had failed to inform the wife of the risks involved and had not advised her to seek independent advice.

Lord Browne-Wilkinson summarised the position as follows:

> "Where one cohabitee has entered into an obligation to stand as surety for the debts of the other cohabitee and the creditor is aware that they are cohabitees:
>
> (1) the surety obligation will be valid and enforceable by the creditor unless the suretyship was procured by the undue influence, misrepresentation or other legal wrong of the principal debtor;
>
> (2) if there has been undue influence, misrepresentation or other legal wrong by the principal debtor, unless the creditor has taken reasonable steps to satisfy himself that the surety entered into the obligation freely and in knowledge of the true facts, the creditor will be unable to enforce the surety obligation because he will be fixed with constructive notice of the surety's right to set aside the transaction;

(3) unless there are special exceptional circumstances, a creditor will have taken such reasonable steps to avoid being fixed with constructive notice if the creditor warns the surety (at a meeting not attended by the principal debtor) of the amount of her [or his] potential liability and of the risks involved and advises the surety to take independent legal advice."

The above procedures have been subject to interpretation in later cases. In *Massey v Midland Bank Plc*, CA, 1995 the Court of Appeal considered that the guidance requirements in O'Brien should not be applied mechanically. A similar approach was taken in *Banco Exterior Internacional v Mann*, CA, 1995. However, in *Credit Lyonnaise Bank Nederland v Burch*, CA, 1997 the court considered that the circumstances of the particular relationship required strict compliance with the O'Brien guidelines. These apparently conflicting approaches caused much uncertainty.

An attempt at reconciliation and further refinement of the *O'Brien* principles has been made by the *House of Lords in Royal Bank of Scotland Plc v Etridge* (No.2), HL, 2001. For the future, a bank seeking to enforce a charge against a surety wife should insist the wife attends a private meeting with a representative of the bank at which she should be told of the extent of her liability as surety, warned of the risk she runs and urged to take independent advice. In exceptional cases, the bank, to be safe, must insist that the wife be separately advised.

The content of the independent legal advice the solicitor advising the wife should give was set out. The solicitor should obtain from the bank any relevant information needed to give the advice. It is not necessary that the solicitor should act only for the wife. He should consider whether there are any conflicts of duty or interest and what are the best interests of the wife. The solicitor is not the bank's agent and in the normal case the bank is entitled to proceed on the assumption that he has done his job properly.

There is no rational cut-off to the type of relationship covered by the *O'Brien* principle. The House of Lords considered that the way forward was to regard banks as "put on inquiry" in every case where the relationship between the surety and the debtor was non-commercial.

BARS TO RELIEF

Where a contract is voidable for duress or undue influence, relief (i.e. rescission) may be barred by: (i) affirmation of the contract by the weaker party after the undue pressure or presumptive relationship has terminated; and (ii) where a third party acquires rights in the subject-matter of the contract, bona fide and for value.

11. ILLEGAL AND VOID CONTRACTS

As a general proposition, the courts will not enforce contracts whose purpose is illegal; this includes not only agreements that are criminal in intent but those that are regarded as injurious to society in the wider sense. In addition, there is a distinction between contracts which are actually illegal and those which are void.

ILLEGAL CONTRACTS

Contracts illegal by statute

A contract may be expressly forbidden by a statutory provision. For example, in *Re Mahmoud and Ispahani*, CA, 1921, by delegated legislation it was forbidden to buy or sell linseed without obtaining a licence. The defendant buyer fraudulently stated that he possessed a licence but was held not liable in an action for non-delivery by the innocent seller. The contract was expressly forbidden.

The prohibition may be implied as in *Cope v Rowlands* (1836) where a statute required that persons acting as stockbroker must obtain a licence, or forfeit £25. The claimant did brokerage work for the defendant without a licence. In the absence of an express prohibition, the brokerage contract was held impliedly illegal since the object of the licences was to protect the public. Alternatively, the court may construe the contract and consider that the prohibition was introduced for an administrative purpose and not to forbid the contract in question; in *Learoyd v Bracken* (1894), a statute required a stockbroker dealing in shares to issue a stamped contract note, or forfeit £20. It was held that a broker who failed to comply was entitled to recover his commission; "the object of the Act was not to vitiate the contract . . . but to impose a penalty . . . for the protection of the revenue," per Lopes L.J. In modern statutes, the line is difficult to draw, as illustrated by *Archbolds (Freightage) Ltd v S. Spanglett Ltd*, CA, 1961.

It is necessary, before considering the effects of illegality (below), to distinguish between a contract that is, (i) illegal as formed; and (ii) one that is illegal as performed. In the case of (i), the very creation of the contract is forbidden, as in *Re Mahmoud and Cope v Rowlands* (above). In the case of (ii), the contract is lawful in its formation but performed by the parties in a manner that is illegal, as in *Ashmore, Benson, Pease Co Ltd v A.V. Dawson Ltd*, CA, 1973. Here, the claimants contracted with the defendant hauliers to carry a 25-ton load. The defendants used articulated lorries which by law were not permitted to carry more than 20 tons; the contract was held illegal in its performance. However, where the illegality is merely incidental to the performance of the contract, the contract may not be illegal at all; *St John Shipping Corp v Joseph Rank Ltd* (1957). For example, in *Shaw v Groom*, CA, 1970, a rent book issued by a landlord failed to provide all the details required by statute. This did not prevent the landlord recovering arrears of rent from the tenant. The test would appear to be whether the illegality in the course of performance affects the "core" of the contract.

Contracts Illegal at common law on the grounds of public policy

Certain contracts are regarded as illegal at common law on the grounds that, being injurious to society, they are contrary to public policy. Others, regarded as less damaging, are merely void (see below). It is questionable whether it is open to the courts to invent new heads of public policy. The contracts are as follows:

(1) Contracts to commit a crime, tort or fraud. Such a contract is illegal; examples include a contract between two highwaymen to ambush a coach (*Everet v Williams* (1725)), a contract to publish a libel (*Apthorp v Neville Co* (1907)) and a contract to purchase shares at inflated prices and thereby rig the market (*Scott v Brown, Doering, McNab Co*, CA, 1892).

(2) Contracts promoting sexual immorality. A contract which directly or indirectly promotes such a purpose is illegal, such as where a prostitute agrees to hire a carriage for the purposes of her trade; *Pearce v Brooks* (1866). The modern tendency is for the courts to look more benignly on agreements which contemplate stable extra-marital relations, as in *Somma v Hazlehurst* (1979) where an unmarried couple occupied a room but the contract was not struck down on the grounds of public policy.

(3) Contracts prejudicial to public safety. The principal examples of contracts illegal on this ground are: trading with an enemy alien in wartime, and contracts to perform acts

which are illegal in a friendly foreign country; *Foster v Driscoll* (1921).

(4) Contracts prejudicial to the administration of justice. As a general rule, a contract which involves stifling a prosecution is illegal and where an arrestable offence is concealed, a crime is thereby committed; Criminal Law Act 1967, s.5(1). However, there is authority that "private" offences such as assault may be lawfully compromised (*McGregor v McGregor*, CA, 1888), but the principle may not apply if the offence is a matter of public concern; *Keir v Leeman* (1846). Agreements tending to defeat the bankruptcy laws have been held illegal; *Elliot v Richardson* (1870).

(5) Contracts tending to promote corruption in public life. A contract to procure a public office or title will be illegal; *Parkinson v College of Ambulance* (1925).

(6) Contracts to defraud the revenue. A contract which has as its objective the defrauding of the national or local revenue is illegal; *Miller v Karlinski*, CA, 1945.

Before considering the effects of illegality (below), it should be noted that the distinction between contracts illegal as formed and illegal as performed, discussed above, also applies to contracts illegal on the grounds of public policy.

Effects of illegality

The first matter to be considered here is the state of mind of the parties. If the contract is illegal as formed (e.g. a contract to commit a crime or a contract expressly forbidden by statute), neither party will be able to sue or acquire rights under the contract. This is so even where the contract on the face of it appears to be legal but there is a common intention to achieve an illegal purpose. Where the contract is legal as formed but one party (and not the other) intends to exploit the contract for an illegal purpose, the innocent party may be able to sue on the contract; *Oom v Bruce* (1810).

The effects of illegality differ according to whether the contract is illegal as formed or illegal as performed.

1. Contract illegal as formed.   The effects are as follows:

(1) The contract is void and therefore neither party can sue upon it, *ex turpi causa non oritur actio* (no right of action arises from a base cause). It may be possible to circum-

vent this rule by bringing an action in misrepresentation; *Shelley v Paddock*, CA, 1980.

(2) Money paid or property transferred under the contract is not recoverable; *Taylor v Chester* (1869). There are certain exceptions to this rule. First, where the party seeking recovery does not have to base his or her action on the illegal contract. Thus, where the claimants transferred machine tools to the defendants under hire-purchase contracts which were illegal, the defendants were held liable (in conversion) for having sold some of the tools. The wrongful sale had terminated the hire-purchase contracts and the claimants' action was brought as owner; *Bowmakers Ltd v Barnet Instruments Ltd*, CA, 1945, *Saunders v Edwards* (1987) and *Tinsley v Milligan*, HL, 1993.

Secondly, where the parties have both participated in the illegal transaction but are not *in pari delicto* (not equally in the wrong), the less guilty party may be allowed to recover. This may be the case where the object of the statute is to protect a class of persons and the claimant is within the class: e.g. a tenant who pays an illegal premium may recover it; *Kiriri Cotton Co Ltd v Dewani*, PC, 1960. Thirdly, where the claimant repents before the illegal purpose has been fully performed, they may be allowed to recover; *Taylor v Bowers*, CA, 1876.

(3) Related transactions will also be void. In *Fisher v Bridges* (1854), a purchaser, who had bought land for an illegal purpose, executed a deed in respect of the balance of the purchase price. It was held no action lay on the deed as it was collateral to an illegal contract of sale. Where a third party enters into such a collateral contract his or her rights may depend upon the state of his or her knowledge as to the illegality; *Spector v Ageda* (1971).

2. Illegal as performed. Where the contract is lawful as formed, but where one party intends to exploit the contract to achieve an illegal purpose (i.e. one party is innocent and the other guilty), the position is as follows:

(1) The guilty party cannot sue on the contract for damages; *Cowan v Milbourn* (1867);

(2) Money or property transferred by the guilty party cannot be recovered back by him or her unless the guilty party does not need to base his or her action on the illegal contract;

(3) The guilty party may be able to sue on a collateral contract that the main contract would be legally performed. In *Strongman Ltd v Sincock*, CA, 1955, the claimant builders carried out works under a contract with an architect. The architect had promised to obtain the necessary licences but failed to do so. The claimants were unable to sue on the main contract because of the illegality, nevertheless the architect was held liable under a collateral contract based on his promise. The innocent party, on the other hand, has full contractual remedies available to him or her, including the right to recover back money or property transferred.

CONTRACTS VOID BY STATUTE

Certain contracts are expressly declared to be void by statute. The most notable examples are wagering contracts (rendered void by the Gaming Act 1845) and restrictive trading agreements (controlled by the Competition Act 1998). Individual resale price maintenance agreements are considered in Chapter 12.

CONTRACTS VOID AT COMMON LAW

Certain contracts are void at common law on the grounds of public policy:

(1) Contracts to oust the jurisdiction of the courts. A contract is void in so far as it purports to deprive the courts of a jurisdiction which they otherwise would have, e.g. an agreement by a wife not to apply to the divorce court for maintenance is contrary to public policy; *Bennett v Bennett*, CA, 1952. The wife in such circumstances is not prevented from applying for maintenance; *Hyman v Hyman*, HL, 1929.

(2) Contracts prejudicial to the status of marriage. A contract is void where it restricts the person's freedom to marry (unless the restriction is mutual); *Lowe v Peers* (1786). An agreement between spouses for a possible future separation is void, as is a marriage brokerage contract (an agreement to procure the marriage of another); *Hermann v Charlesworth*, CA, 1905.

(3) Contracts in restraint of trade. Contracts which are subject to the restraint of trade doctrine are prima facie void. The subject has generated more litigation than the other heads of public policy and will be dealt with more fully below.

CONTRACTS IN RESTRAINT OF TRADE

Certain contracts which impose a restriction on a person's right to carry on a trade or profession fall within the restraint of trade doctrine.

All contracts falling within the doctrine are contrary to public policy and prima facie void, unless they can be regarded as reasonable as between the parties and as regards the public interest.

The burden of proving that, as between the parties, the restraint is reasonable, lies on the promisee; the burden of proving that, as far as the public interest is concerned, the restraint is unreasonable, lies on the promisor. Reasonableness is considered as at the time of the agreement.

The following transactions fall within the doctrine.

1. Agreements between employer and employee relating to the subsequent occupation of the employee An agreement imposing a restriction on the employee after leaving an employer will only be reasonable between the parties if there is some proprietary interest of the employer meriting protection, i.e. trade secrets or business connection. The restriction must be no wider than reasonably necessary to protect such interest. Such restrictions must be express and will not be implied by the court; *Faccenda Chicken Ltd v Fowler*, CA, 1987.

In *Forster v Suggett* (1918), the defendant was employed as works manager of the claimant's glass works. He agreed that for five years after termination of employment with the claimants, he would not divulge any secret manufacturing process learnt during employment, nor would he work in the glass industry in the United Kingdom. It was held that the restraint was reasonable to protect the claimant's legitimate interest and was enforceable.

An employer may similarly protect his or business connection if the employee is in a position of influence to subsequently entice away established customers, providing the restraint is no wider than reasonably necessary; *Herbert Morris Ltd v Saxelby*, HL, 1916. Restraints have been upheld against a milk roundsman, brewery manager and a solicitor's clerk, but disallowed against a bookmaker's manager who had no personal contact with customers.

Occasionally, the courts are prepared to recognise other interests as meriting protection, apart from trade secrets and business connection. For example, in *Greig v Insole* (1978), a professional cricketer sought to challenge a ban on cricketers who had joined a commercial "World Series". Slade J. recognised that the governing bodies of cricket had a legitimate interest in ensuring that the game was properly administered; however, in the circumstances the ban was unreasonable. In this case, however, it should be noted that there was no contract between the cricketer and the governing bodies.

The restriction must also be reasonable as regards both area and duration. In *Mason v Provident Clothing Co Ltd*, HL, 1913, a restriction on a canvasser was held void as the area of restraint (25 miles of London) was one thousand times larger than the area of employment, and in *Fitch v Dewes* (1921), a life-long restraint on a solicitor's managing clerk not to work within seven miles of Tamworth was held to be reasonable in the circumstances.

Exceptionally, agreements between an employer and employee will be held unreasonable as regards the public interest, i.e. where the community will be deprived of a valuable skill; *Wyatt v Kreglinger and Fernau*, CA, 1933. The courts are also prepared to invalidate indirect means of restraining employees; thus in *Kores Manufacturing Co Ltd v Kolok Manufacturing Co Ltd*, CA, 1959, two companies manufacturing similar products agreed that neither firm would employ a person who had been employed by the other in the previous five years. The agreement was held to be unreasonably wide as it failed to distinguish between employees privy to trade secrets and those who were not.

A covenant purporting to restrain an employee from working for a competitor will be extinguished where the employer commits a repudiatory breach terminating the contract; *Rock Refrigeration Ltd v Jones*, CA, 1997.

2. Agreements between the buyer and seller of a business.

Restraints imposed upon the seller of a business to restrict competition are more readily upheld than restraints upon employees (above) but are generally subject to the same principles.

There must be a proprietary interest in need of protection; only the actual business sold is entitled to protection. In *British Reinforced Concrete Co v Schleff* (1921), the claimant firm made and sold "BRC" road reinforcements. The defendants sold, but did not make "Loop" road reinforcements. The claimants bought the defendants' business, the defendants covenanting not to compete in the manufacture and sale of road reinforcements in the United Kingdom for a specified period. It was held that the restraint was unreasonably wide as it extended to manufacture instead of being confined to sale. The case also illustrates that a restraint on competition per se is void. For the same reason, a restriction which purports to restrain a business not actually carried on will be void: *Malt and Sake Brewing Co Ltd v Vancouver Breweries Ltd*, PC, 1934.

3. Agreements between manufacturers to restrict output and fix prices. Such agreements are prima facie void at common law but the courts have been prepared to uphold where reasonable, e.g. to avoid a glut on the market; *English Hop Growers v Dering*, CA, 1928. In fact such agreements are now almost entirely subject to statutory control under the Competition Act 1998.

4. Exclusive dealing agreements. "Solus" agreements, whereby a garage agrees to purchase all its supply of petrol from one oil company, are within the doctrine of restraint of trade and are prima facie void.

In *Esso Petroleum Co Ltd v Harper's Garage (Stourport) Ltd*, HL, 1968, the owner of two garages agreed, inter alia, to sell only Esso's petrol, in return for a rebate on the price per gallon. On one of the garages, the tie was to last for nearly four-and-a-half years and on the other it was to last for 21 years, being contained in this case in a mortgage of the premises to Esso. The House of Lords upheld the four and a half year agreement although the agreement for 21 years was held to be unreasonable and void as being longer than necessary to protect Esso's interests, i.e. the continuity and stability of their marketing operation.

However, if a trader, when purchasing or leasing new premises, covenants with the vendor or lessor (in the conveyance or lease) to buy only the latter's products, and then goes into possession, the exclusive dealing tie is outside the restraint of trade doctrine; *Harper's* Case. This would apply to a person who buys or takes a lease of a public house or garage subject to a tie; the reason is that the person has surrendered no freedom previously enjoyed.

The approach of the courts to exclusive dealing ties is illustrated by *Alec Lobb (Garages) Ltd v Total Oil Ltd*, CA, 1985.

The claimants, whilst in financial difficulties, leased their garage to the defendant oil company for 51 years at a premium of £35,000. The defendants sub-leased it back to the plaintiffs for 21 years at an annual rent of £2,250, with a mutual right to break at seven or 14 years. The sub-lease contained a solus tie whereby the claimants agreed to sell only the defendants' petrol. The Court of Appeal held that the lease and lease-back were subject to the restraint of trade doctrine but the tie was valid as being reasonable in the circumstances. The principal purpose of the agreement was as a financial rescue operation from which the claimants benefited as they received ample consideration (£35,000) for the lease and they were free to exercise the break clause after seven or 14 years.

Exclusive service agreements, such as where, for example, a songwriter agrees to provide his services for a music publisher for a period of time, are within the restraint of trade doctrine, (i.e. prima facie void) if oppressive and one-sided; *Schroeder Music Publishing Co Ltd v Macaulay*, HL, 1974.

Effects of the contract being void

The effects discussed below relate to contracts void at common law and will apply by analogy to contracts void by statute unless the statute in question has special provisions dealing with the matter.

The effects are as follows:

(1) The contract is void in so far as it contravenes public policy. In *Wallis v Day* (1837), a contract of employment contained a provision which was alleged to be a void restraint of trade. This did not prevent the claimant being able to recover arrears of salary. It follows from this that subsequent or collateral transactions are not necessarily void unless they relate solely to that part of the original transaction that is itself void.

(2) Money paid or property transferred is recoverable. Authority for this proposition is to be found in *Hermann v Charlesworth*, CA, 1905.

(3) Severance. Severance is the power of the court to remove a void provision in a contract and enforce the remainder. The power exists in the case of void contracts and there is authority that an illegal contract may be subjected to severance; *Carney v Herbert*, PC, 1985.

Severance will not be possible if it would eliminate the whole or substantially the whole of the consideration given by a party to the contract; *Wyatt v Kreglinger and Fernau*, CA, 1933. It may be possible to sever in the sense of removing the void part of a promise and enforcing the rest. This will be possible providing the severance does not alter the meaning of the contract in any way. In *Goldsoll v Goldman*, CA, 1915, the defendant sold a jewellery business to the claimant, the defendant covenanting that he would not deal in real or imitation jewellery in the United Kingdom or in other specified foreign places. The restraint as to the latter was too wide in the circumstances, as was the reference to real jewellery since the business dealt only in imitation jewellery in the United Kingdom. The void restrictions were severed leaving a valid contract in restraint of trade.

However, in *Attwood v Lamont*, CA, 1920, the defendant was employed as a tailoring cutter for the claimant, a general outfitter. The defendant covenanted not to subsequently engage in a number of trades carried on by the claimant's business, including tailor, milliner, draper, hatter and haberdasher within 10 miles radius. The court refused to sever so as to leave the tailoring restriction valid; the covenant formed a single indivisible covenant for the protection of the claimant's entire business. It was not a series of covenants for the protection of each department of the claimant's business. The whole covenant was therefore void.

It should further be noted that, where severance applies, the court will not redraft the covenant in any way, thus applying the so-called "blue pencil test". The court will merely strike out the offending words; what is left must make sense without further additions.

An alternative to the doctrine of severance in restraint of trade cases is the so-called "flexible" or non-literal approach to construction. In *Littlewoods Organisation Ltd v Harris*, CA, 1978 Harris was a director of the mail order firm, Littlewoods. He entered into a restraint clause whereby he agreed not to work for the GUS group of companies for 12 months after leaving Littlewoods. Harris had acquired confidential information in relation to Littlewoods mail order catalogue. GUS were Littlewoods' main rival in the domestic mail order business, however, GUS operated world-wide and their business was not confined to mail order, whereas Littlewoods only operated in the United Kingdom. The Court of Appeal held that although the clause, on its literal wording, was too wide, by construing the clause with reference to circumstances existing when the contract was made, it was possible to limit it to those matters it was clearly intended to protect, i.e. the mail order business in the United Kingdom. The clause was therefore a valid restraint of trade. As a consequence of the Littlewoods decision, the court may reach a different conclusion dependent upon whether it adopts the literal or flexible approach to construction. This dilemma is illustrated by apparently conflicting subsequent decisions, e.g. *J A Mont (UK) Ltd v Mills*, CA, 1993 and *Hanover Insurance Brokers Ltd v Schapiro*, CA, 1994.

12. PRIVITY OF CONTRACT

The rule of privity means that, in general, a person who is not privy to a contract, that is, a third party, can neither sue nor be sued on that contract.

Where the rule prevents the burden of a contract being imposed on a third party, it is both sensible and just. Thus, in *Dunlop Pneumatic Tyre Co v Selfridge Co Ltd*, HL, 1915, the claimants sold tyres to Dew and Co, wholesale distributors, on terms that Dew and Co would obtain an undertaking from retailers that they would not sell below the claimant's list price. Dew and Co sold some of the tyres to the defendants, who retailed them below list price and the claimants sought an injunction and damages. The action failed because although there was a contract between the claimants and Dew and Co, the defendants were not a party to it and so the obligation they sought to impose on the defendants was unenforceable.

The rule of privity is less easy to justify where a contract between A and B is intended to confer a benefit on a third party, C. In such a situation C cannot enforce the contract because (i) they are not privy to the contract between A and B; and (ii) C has not provided consideration (see *Tweddle v Atkinson*, Chapter 4). A classic example of this situation is *Beswick v Beswick*, HL, 1968, discussed below. Legislative reform to allow the third party to sue was first mooted 60 years ago and then in 1996 the Law Commission put forward draft legislation, this, after some amendment, became the Contracts (Rights of Third Parties) Act 1999. The provisions of the Act are dealt with below. The rule of privity is subject to a number of exceptions and various attempts have been made to evade the doctrine, not always successfully. The established exceptions will be considered first.

ESTABLISHED EXCEPTIONS

Statutory exceptions

There are a number of statutory exceptions, of which the most important are as follows: under the Law of Property Act 1925, s.136, it is possible to assign rights arising under a contract; under the Bills of Exchange Act 1882, s.29, a third party may sue on a bill of exchange or cheque and under the Married Woman's Property Act 1882, s.11, as amended, a spouse may obtain the benefit of a contract of life assurance which is made for the benefit of the other spouse.

Agency

Agency is a major common law exception to the doctrine of privity. A contract of agency arises where one person (the principal) appoints an agent to enter into contracts on his or her behalf with third parties. As a general rule, the principal, even if undisclosed, may sue the third party. An example of agency being used to circumvent the privity rule is to be seen in *N.Z. Shipping Co Ltd v A.M. Satterthwaite Co Ltd*, PC, 1975 (see Chapter 7).

Collateral contract

The collateral contract device, whilst not strictly an exception, may be used to evade the privity rule. In *Shanklin Pier Ltd v Detel Products Ltd* (1951), the claimants employed contractors to repaint their pier and specified that the defendants' (i.e. *Detel's*) paint was to be used. The defendants had previously represented to the claimants that the paint would last from seven to 10 years. The defendants sold the paint to the contractors and it was used but it only lasted three months. Although the claimants could not sue on the contract for the sale of the paint, to which they were not a party, it was held that the claimants could sue the defendants on a collateral contract arising from their promise as to the longevity of the paint. The claimants' consideration to enforce this promise consisted of their causing the contractors to enter into a contract to buy paint from the defendants.

Covenants which run with the land

The position in land law is that burdens imposed on land may in certain circumstances "run with the land" and be enforceable against subsequent owners; *Smith and Snipes Hall Farm v River Douglas Catchment Board*, CA, 1949. Similarly, covenants in leases may, providing certain conditions are satisfied, likewise run with the land. In equity, under the doctrine of *Tulk v Moxhay* (1848), a restrictive covenant may run with the land; thus if A buys land from B, promising not to build thereon, and A later sells to C, C may be bound by the restriction. For the restriction to be enforceable against C, two major conditions must be satisfied: (i) C must have had notice of the restriction at the time of purchase; and (ii) B must have retained land capable of benefiting from the restriction.

Restrictions on price

At common law, suppliers were prevented from restricting the price at which goods were resold by the doctrine of privity (see *Dunlop v Selfridge*, above).

The position is now regulated by statute. By virtue of the Competition Act 1998, any attempt by a supplier to fix a minimum price at which goods are resold is void.

ATTEMPTS TO EVADE PRIVITY

Restrictions upon the use of chattels

The question has arisen whether the principle in *Tulk v Moxhay* (above) may be applied to personalty, so as to render a restriction upon the use of a chattel enforceable against a subsequent owner who is not party to the original contract.

In *Lord Strathcona Steamship Co v Dominion Coal Co*, PC, 1926, the respondents chartered the ship SS. Strathcona for use on the St. Lawrence River for several summer seasons. During the period of the charterparty, the ship was sold to the appellants who took with notice of the charter. They subsequently refused to permit the respondents to use the ship in accordance with the charterparty. An injunction was granted to restrain the appellants from using the ship in a manner inconsistent with the charterparty. The Privy Council in this case placed much reliance on the principle in *Tulk v Moxhay*. This, however, is open to the objection that the charterers lacked the proprietary interest necessary to enforce a restrictive covenant under *Tulk v Moxhay*. Further, in *Clore v Theatrical Properties Ltd*, CA, 1936, the Court of Appeal said that the *Strathcona* decision should be confined to the particular case of the charterparty of a ship, and in *Port Line Ltd v Ben Line Steamers Ltd* (1958), Diplock J. considered that *Strathcona* was wrongly decided.

In fact the case has met with some recent approval, although not on the restrictive covenant theory. In *Swiss Bank Corp v Lloyds Bank Ltd* (1979), Browne-Wilkinson J. took the view that the appellants in *Strathcona* were in the position of constructive trustees, or alternatively, the principle in the case was the "counterpart in equity" of the tort of knowingly interfering with contractual relations. Although this may be indicative of the way the law will develop, as things stand at present, *Strathcona*, even if correctly decided, is of limited application.

The trust device

One means of evading the doctrine of privity is to show that, where A contracts with B to confer a benefit on C, one of the contracting parties, say B, is holding their contractual rights on trust for C. In such a case, C may be able to ask B to sue as trustee; in the event of a refusal, C may bring proceedings joining the trustee as co-defendant. The trust device in this context can be traced to *Gregory and Parker v Williams* (1817) and had become firmly established by the time of *Les Affrêteurs Réunis SA v Walford*, HL, 1919. In this case, Walford, a broker, arranged a charterparty between shipowners and charterers. The charterparty contained a term by which the shipowners promised to pay Walford three per cent. commission on the value of the hire. Although Walford was not privy to the contract between the charterers and the shipowners, the House of Lords held that the charterers were to be regarded as trustees for Walford and they could therefore enforce payment of the commission against the shipowners.

No formal words are required to create such a trust but there must be the intention to create a trust, although "an intention to provide benefits for someone else and pay them does not of itself give rise to a trusteeship," per Romer L.J. in *Green v Russell*, CA, 1959. The device depends largely on the readiness of the court to construe a trust and many of the decided cases are inconsistent. The judicial tide seems to have turned against the trust device in *Re Schebsman*, CA, 1943, where Schebsman's employers agreed to pay him an annual sum, or, if he died, payment would be made to his wife and daughter. The Court of Appeal, in holding that there was no trust, were influenced by the fact that Schebsman and his employers were at liberty to vary consensually the terms of the agreement; this would not have been possible had the contract created a trust.

It is noteworthy that in *Beswick v Beswick*, HL, 1968, (see below) where the facts were not dissimilar to *Re Schebsman*, the Court of Appeal were of the view that no trust could be inferred in favour of the third party and the matter was not canvassed before the House of Lords.

Section 56 of the Law of Property Act 1925

Section 56(1) of the Law of Property Act 1925 provides that a person may acquire an interest in land or other property, or the benefit of a covenant relating to land or other property, although not actually named as a party in the conveyance or other document. Further, s.205(1) provides that, unless the context otherwise requires, the word "property" means any interest in real or personal property.

Liberally interpreted, these provisions could present a means of evading the doctrine of privity, particularly if the reference to "other property" could embrace contractual rights. The effect of the provisions arose in *Beswick v Beswick*, HL, 1968. Here, a coal merchant agreed to sell his business to his nephew, who in return agreed to pay a weekly sum to his uncle, and after the uncle's death a weekly sum would be payable to the uncle's widow. Ultimately, the widow brought an action against the nephew for arrears of the weekly sum and for specific performance of the agreement. She sued (i) as administratrix of her deceased husband's estate; and (ii) in her personal capacity, relying on s.56(1).

The Court of Appeal held that she was entitled as administratrix to an order of specific performance; a majority of the court found that she could also succeed in her personal capacity by virtue of s.56(1). On appeal to the House of Lords, it was held that her claim as administratrix was good and she was entitled to specific performance since damages would be an inadequate remedy. Her personal claim should fail as s.56(1) was limited to transactions involving realty; there was a presumption that the Law of Property Act 1925, being a consolidating Act, did not fundamentally alter the common law by a "sidewind".

RIGHT TO CLAIM DAMAGES

Where A contracts with B to confer a benefit on C, we have seen that although C has no rights at common law because of privity, C may acquire rights if the contract creates a trust in favour of C, or alternatively if one of the parties to the contract contracts as C's agent.

In the absence of either of these, at common law, the only means by which the contract may be enforced is if one of the contracting parties themselves sues. The problem here is that in many cases damages will be the usual remedy, unless specific performance is ordered, as in *Beswick v Beswick*. In strict theory the damages will only be nominal since the claimant, as a contracting party, will have suffered no loss.

In *Jackson v Horizon Holidays Ltd*, CA, 1975, the claimant contracted with the defendants for a holiday for himself and his family which turned out to be disastrous. The claimant recovered substantial damages to cover not only his own disappointment, but also that of his wife and children. Lord Denning M.R. was of the view, relying on dictum in *Lloyds v Harper*, CA, 1880, that the contracting party in such circumstances can recover substantial damages to cover the third party's loss. This view was corrected by the House of Lords in *Woodar Investment Development Ltd v Wimpey Construction U.K. Ltd*, HL, 1980 as being too wide. The decision in Jackson was justified by the House on the basis the claimant's damages reflected his own disappointment at the ruined family holiday or as a special category of case where contracts are arranged by one person for a group.

Another exception to the general rule was allowed in *Linden Gardens Trust Ltd v Lanesta Sludge Disposals Ltd*, HL, 1994. X employed Y to carry out work on his land, in circumstances where it was understood that X was likely to transfer the property to Z. The work of Y was defective and in breach of contract. Although X no longer had any interest in the property, the House of Lords awarded substantial damages; per Lord Browne-Wilkinson, it seems proper "to treat the parties as having entered the contract on the footing that [the original owner] would be entitled to enforce the contractual rights for the benefit of those who suffered from defective performance". Nevertheless, in *Alfred McAlpine Construction Ltd v Panatown Ltd*, HL, 2000 the House of Lords debarred the employer in a building contract, by reason of the fact that it was not the owner of the land, from recovering substantial damages where the owner had a direct right to sue the contractor. Thus, there was no necessity to depart from the general rule that substantial damages cannot be recovered by a promisee suffering no loss.

CONTRACTS (RIGHTS OF THIRD PARTIES) ACT 1999

The fundamental change to the common law brought about by the Act is to be found in s.1(1) and 1(2). Section 1(1) of the Act states:

"Subject to the provisions of this Act, a person who is not a party to the contract (a 'third party') may in his own right enforce a term of the contract if—

(a) the contract provides that he may, or
(b) subject to subsection (2), the term purports to confer a benefit on him."

However, subsection (2) provides that s.1(1)(b) above will "not apply if on a proper construction of the contract it appears that the parties did not intend the term to be enforceable by the third party."

In the first reported case under the Act, *Nisshin Shipping Co Ltd v Cleaves*, 2003, it was held that the effect of s.1(2) was to provide that s.1(1)(b) was disapplied if on a proper construction it appeared that the parties did not intend third party enforcement—if the contract was neutral on the question, s.1(2) did not disapply s.1(1)(b).

The third party must be expressly identified in the contract by name, as a member of a class or as answering a particular description but need not be in existence when the contract is entered into (s.1(3)).

Once it is established that the third party has an enforceable right, the Act makes available to him or her any remedy available to a party to the contract, e.g. damages, injuction or specific performance (s.1(5)). Likewise, they may take the benefit of an exclusion or limitation clause (s.1(6)).

Variation and rescission

The parties to the contract may not, unless the agreement otherwise provides, rescind or vary the beneficial term to the detriment of the third party if:

(1) the third party has communicated, by words or conduct, his assent to the relevant term to the promisor;
(2) the promisor is aware that the third party has relied on the relevant term; or
(3) the promisor can reasonably be expected to have foreseen that the third party would rely on the relevant term and the third party has in fact relied on it (ss.2(1), (2) and (3)).

Defences

Section 3 provides that the promisor may, unless the contract otherwise provides, raise against the third party any defence or set-off that could have been raised against the promisee. The above provision means that the third party will be no more able to enforce a void, discharged or unenforceable contract than the promisee could.

The Act also provides (s.3(4)) that the promisor may rely on defences, set-offs or counterclaims against the third party which do not arise from the contract itself but from previous dealings. A third party can only rely on any exclusion or limitation clause if he could have done so had he been a party to the contract (s.3(6)).

Finally, s.5 provides that where the promisee has recovered damages from the promisor in respect of the third party's loss, the court shall reduce any award to the third party to take account of the sum already recovered.

Exceptions

Section 6 prescribes a number of contracts which are specifically excepted from the provisions of the Act. These include bills of exchange and promissory notes, terms in contracts of employment against an employee, terms in contracts for the carriage of goods by sea other than clauses of exclusion or limitation (and certain other contracts of carriage other than clauses of exclusion and limitation). This means that a third party may rely on an exclusion clause without having to rely on the agency device in *N.Z. Shipping Co Ltd v A.M. Satterthwaite Co Ltd*, PC, 1975.

Effect of the legislation

Section 7(1) provides that the Act "does not affect any right or remedy of a third party that exists or is available apart from this Act"; thus the Act does not replace any of the established judicial exceptions to privity. It may mean, however, that the third parties in cases such as *Beswick v Beswick* and (possibly) *Jackson v Horizon Holidays* will be able to bring an action in their own right. Nevertheless, as we have seen, it will be perfectly possible for the parties to the contract to exclude the operation of the statute.

13. DISCHARGE OF CONTRACT

A contract may be discharged under the doctrine of frustration, or by breach, or by agreement or by the contract being performed. These matters will be dealt with in turn.

FRUSTRATION

Under the doctrine of frustration, a contract may be automatically discharged if, during the currency of the contract, and without the fault of either party, some event occurs which renders further performance an impossibility, renders it illegal or brings about a radical change in the circumstances so that the contract becomes something essentially different from that which was originally undertaken.

Juristic basis

It is necessary to establish the juristic basis of the doctrine in order to apply the correct legal test for discovering whether the contract has been frustrated. There are two main theories.

1. Radical change in the obligation. This test was favoured by the majority of the House of Lords in *Davis Contractors Ltd v Fareham U.D.C.*, HL, 1956. Per Lord Radcliffe: ". . . there must be such a change in the significance of the obligation that the thing undertaken would, if performed, be a different thing from that contracted for". The test is objective, discharge occurs automatically upon the frustrating event and does not depend on any repudiation by the parties.

2. Implied term theory. This theory stems from *Taylor v Caldwell*, HL, 1863 and *F.A. Tamplin S.S. v Anglo Mexican Petroleum*, HL, 1916. In these cases it was said that the contract was to be construed as being subject to an implied term that the parties shall be excused if performance were to become impossible by virtue of some event which is the fault of neither party. The theory has been criticised as artificial and the first of the two theories is now generally preferred.

Frustrating events

The situations in which a contract might become frustrated cannot be exhaustively listed but the cases may be categorised under the following heads.

1. Impossibility. A contract may become impossible to perform where the subject-matter is destroyed. In *Taylor v Caldwell* (1863), the claimant agreed to hire a music hall from the defendant for the purpose of holding concerts on specified dates. Before the first of these dates and without the fault of either party, the hall was destroyed by fire. It was held that the contract was discharged by frustration.

Similarly a contract may be frustrated if the subject-matter becomes, through some extraneous cause, unavailable, as where a ship required for the performance of the contract is stranded; *Nickoll and Knight v Ashton Eldridge Co* (1901). The unavailability of a person required for the performance of a contract may similarly frustrate it; *Morgan v Manser* (1948).

Where a particular method of performance becomes impossible, the contract will only be frustrated where the method is essential to the performance of the contract and it was expressly or impliedly stipulated for in the contract itself. In *Tsakiroglou Co Ltd v Noblee Thorl GmbH*, HL, 1962, the closure of the Suez Canal did not frustrate a contract to ship groundnuts despite the fact that the parties anticipated they would be shipped via Suez. The House of Lords refused to imply a term to that effect since the voyage round the Cape was not commercially fundamentally different.

2. Illegality. If, during the currency of the contract, a change in the law renders further performance illegal, the contract will be frustrated. Thus, the outbreak of hostilities may render the further performance of a trading contract illegal as "trading with the enemy".

3. Radical change in the circumstances. Exceptionally, frustration may occur where, due to some extraneous event, further performance, though technically possible, would become something radically different from that originally envisaged by the parties.

In *Krell v Henry*, CA, 1903, the claimant agreed to let a room to the defendant for coronation day. It was understood by both parties that the purpose of the letting was to view the procession. It was held that the cancellation of the coronation frustrated the contract; the viewing of the procession was the "foundation of the contract".

However, in another case, a contract for the hire of a steamboat for viewing the King's naval review and for a cruise around the fleet was held not to be frustrated by the cancellation of the review. The review was not regarded as the foundation of the contract; *Herne Bay Steam Boat Co v Hutton*, CA, 1903.

A contract will not be frustrated where a change of circumstances renders it more onerous to perform but not radically different. In *Davis Contractors Ltd v Fareham U.D.C.*, HL, 1956, the House of Lords refused to hold a building contract frustrated where, because of labour shortages, the work took three times longer than had been agreed.

The courts have traditionally been reluctant to apply the doctrine of frustration to leaseholds, as a lease creates an estate in the land. In *Cricklewood Property and Investment Trust Ltd v Leighton's Investment Trust Ltd*, HL, 1945, the House of Lords was evenly divided on the matter, but in *National Carriers Ltd v Panalpina (Northern) Ltd*, HL, 1981 the House decided, by a majority, that a lease could be frustrated, although only very rarely.

Limits to frustration

The courts have imposed certain limits on the doctrine:

(1) Self-induced frustration. Where the alleged "frustrating" event is brought about by the fault of one of the parties, the "frustration" is said to be self-induced and the party at fault will be liable for breach of contract. The contract will not be discharged by frustration. An example is where one party elects to pursue a course of action that renders performance impossible; *Maritime National Fish Ltd v Ocean Trawlers Ltd*, PC, 1935 and *Super Servant Two*, CA, 1990. The onus of proving the frustration is self-induced lies on the party so alleging.

(2) Express provision. A contract may contain an express provision dealing with the possibility of a frustrating event which then in fact occurs. If this is the case, the doctrine of frustration does not apply and the risks are allocated in accordance with the terms of the contract (illegality excepted). Such provisions are construed narrowly; *Metropolitan Water Board v Dick Kerr Co Ltd*, HL, 1918.

(3) Event foreseen. If one party foresaw or should have foreseen the "frustrating" event by reason of his or her own special knowledge, the doctrine of frustration does

not apply and that party will be liable for breach of contract; *Walton Harvey Ltd v Walker and Homfrays Ltd*, CA, 1931. There is authority for the proposition that if both parties foresaw or should have foreseen the event, but made no provision in the contract to deal with it, the contract may nevertheless be frustrated; *W.J. Tatem Ltd v Gamboa* (1939).

Legal effect of frustration

The effect of frustration is to discharge the contract automatically as to the future, but not to render it void ab initio (cf. the effect of an operative mistake; see Chapter 9).

The result is that, at common law, the rights and liabilities of the parties existing before the frustrating event are preserved, thus "the loss lies where it falls". The harsh consequence of this at common law was that money paid by one party to the other before the frustrating event could not be recovered, and money payable before the frustration remained payable; *Chandler v Webster*, CA, 1904.

This rigid rule was modified by the House of Lords in *Fibrosa S.A. v Fairbairn Lawson Combe Barbour Ltd*, HL, 1943. Here, an English company agreed to sell machinery to a Polish company, with a deposit of one-third of the purchase price being paid at the time of the agreement. Before any machinery was delivered, war broke out and the contract was frustrated. The House of Lords held, overruling *Chandler v Webster*, that the Polish company were entitled to recover the deposit paid, on the ground of a total failure of consideration (a form of quasi-contract). Money had been paid to secure performance and there had been no performance.

The law was still unsatisfactory in that (i) there was no remedy where the failure of consideration was only partial; and (ii) it did not provide for the situation where the payee had incurred expenses in reliance on the contract (as the English company had done in Fibrosa). These injustices led to legislation.

The Law Reform (Frustrated Contracts) Act 1943

The Act was passed to provide for a just apportionment of losses where a contract is discharged by frustration.

The main provisions of the Act are as follows.

1. Recovery of money paid. Money paid before the frustrating event is recoverable and money payable before the frustrating event ceases to be payable, whether or not there has been a total failure of consideration (s.1(2)).

If, however, the party to whom such sums are paid or are payable incurred expenses before discharge in performance of the contract, the court may award him or her such expenses up to the limit of the money paid or payable before the frustrating event (s.1(2)). It follows that if nothing was paid or payable before discharge, they will be unable to recover expenses, although they may be able to rely on s.1(3) below.

In *Gamerco SA v ICM/Fair Warning (Agency) Ltd*, 1995, Garland J said that in calculating the award under s.1(2), there was:

> "no indication in the [Act], the authorities or relevant literature that the court is obliged to incline towards total retention or equal division. Its task is to do justice in a situation which the parties had neither contemplated nor provided for, and to mitigate the possible harshness of allowing all loss to lie where it falls."

2. Valuable benefit. If one party has, by reason of anything done by the other party in performance of the contract, obtained a valuable benefit (other than money) before the frustrating event, they may be ordered to pay a just sum in respect of it (s.1(3)).

In arriving at the sum, the court must consider all the circumstances of the case, in particular whether the benefited party has incurred expenses in the performance of the contract before the time of discharge and the effect, in relation to the benefit, of the circumstances giving rise to the frustration of the contract.

It is likely that s.1(3) was enacted with *Appleby v Myers* (1867) in mind. In that case, the claimants agreed to install machinery in the defendant's factory for £459. When the work was nearly completed, an accidental fire destroyed the factory and all its contents. An action for £419 for work and materials failed; the contract was frustrated and no payment was due at the time of discharge.In fact, it may be doubted whether *Appleby v Myers* would be decided any differently even after the Act of 1943, particularly if the court were to take a narrow view of the meaning of "valuable benefit". This would seem to be confirmed by *B.P. Exploration Co (Libya) v Hunt* (No.2) (1979, affirmed HL, 1983) where Robert Goff J. said;

> "where the services rendered by the [claimant] have an end-product, s.1(3) shows that the value of the end-product is the

benefit. Where a contract is frustrated by a fire which destroys a building on which work has been done, the award will be nil."

3. Scope of the Act. There are certain contracts to which the Act does not apply, including the following:

(1) any charterparty, except time charters and charters by way of demise, or any other contract for the carriage of goods by sea;

(2) contracts of insurance; and

(3) contracts for the sale of specific goods which are frustrated by the goods perishing.

BREACH

A breach of contract will occur where one party fails to fulfil, or intimates that they do not intend to fulfil, their obligations under the contract.

The consequences of the breach of particular types of term has already been considered (see Chapter 6), but for present purposes it should be noted that some breaches entitle the innocent party to sue for damages only; others, more serious, entitle the innocent party, in addition to claiming damages, to treat themselves as discharged from the contract. Serious breaches of this nature are generally described as "repudiatory" breaches. After such a breach, the innocent party has an election; they may decide to accept the breach as a repudiation of the contract or may decide to affirm the contract, i.e. the innocent party is not bound to discharge themselves from the contract. Where they decide to treat the breach as repudiatory, this state of affairs must be communicated to the other party. This communication requires no particular form, "the aggrieved party need not personally . . . notify the repudiating party of his election . . . it is sufficient that the fact of the election comes to the repudiating party's attention" (per Lord Steyn in *Vitol S.A. v Norelf Ltd*, HL, 1996).

In order to establish that a breach of contract amounts to a repudiation, it must be shown that the contract-breaking party has, beyond reasonable doubt, evinced an intention no longer to fulfil his or her part of the contract; *Woodar Investment Developments Ltd v Wimpey Construction (U.K.) Ltd*, HL, 1980.

Anticipatory breach

A breach may occur before performance is due, i.e. where the party effectively intimates that they do not intend to perform their part of the contract. In such a case, the breach is described as an "anticipatory breach". Anticipatory breach may be explicit, as in *Hochster v De La Tour* (1853), where the defendant agreed in April to employ the claimant as a courier commencing June. In May, the defendant informed the claimant that he would not require his services. The claimant's action for damages in May succeeded. Alternatively, it may be implicit, where the defendant by conduct disables themselves from performance, as in *Frost v Knight* (1870). Here, the defendant, having agreed to marry the claimant on his father's death, broke off the engagement during the father's lifetime. It was held that the claimant was at that point entitled to damages.

In both cases, the innocent party has an immediate right of action; they may sue for breach of contract at once (i.e. the innocent party may "accept the repudiation") or they may await the date of performance and hold the other party to the contract. Where the innocent party refuses to accept the repudiation, the contract remains in force and the rights of the innocent party are preserved. The possible consequences of this are illustrated by *White and Carter (Councils) Ltd v McGregor*, HL, 1962 (see Chapter 14).

Refusing to accept a repudiation is not without its risks as the innocent party may lose their right of action if the contract becomes frustrated in the intervening period before performance is due; *Avery v Bowden* (1855).

AGREEMENT

A contract may be discharged or varied by agreement. As a general rule, consideration will be required to render an agreement to discharge or vary valid, and in some cases formalities will be required.

Consideration and formalities

Where a simple contract is executory on both sides, an agreement to discharge or vary the contract provides its own consideration; each party agrees to release the other from his or her outstanding obligations under the contract.

Where a simple contract is executed on one side, a deed is required to effect a valid release of the other party. In the absence of a deed, the other party must provide new consideration (an "accord and satisfaction"). The consideration itself need not be executed but may consist of an executory promise; *Elton Cop Dyeing Co v Broadbent and Son Ltd, CA*, 1919. The same principles apply to a variation.

There are two special cases:

(1) Contracts required to be evidenced in writing. Where the contract is one that requires written evidence to be enforceable (see Chapter 5), the contract may be validly discharged by an oral agreement, with no requirement of written evidence; *Morris v Baron* (1918). Although the oral words suffice to discharge the original agreement, any new agreement substituted in its place will require written evidence, as will any variation of the original agreement.

(2) Contracts by deed. At common law, a contract by deed could only be discharged in the form in which it was made. However, in equity (which now prevails), such a contract may be validly discharged or varied by an oral agreement; *Berry v Berry* (1929).

Rescission, variation and waiver

The parties may intend to discharge, i.e. rescind the original agreement and substitute a new agreement or they may intend to vary the original agreement. There will be rescission if, by their subsequent agreement, the parties alter the original agreement in some fundamental way. If not, there will only be a variation.

We have seen that, in some cases, a variation requires consideration or form. As a result, the common law developed the doctrine of waiver. Whereas a variation involves an alteration in the terms of a contract, a waiver is an indulgence voluntarily given by one party to the other not to insist on the precise mode of performance laid down by the contract. A waiver could take effect without consideration and even without the required formalities for a variation. A common example is where a buyer of goods allows the seller to make late delivery.

At common law, the party seeking the indulgence is not permitted to repudiate the waiver and set up the original terms of the contract; *Levey Co v Goldberg* (1922). The waiver is binding on the party who grants it; *Hartley v Hymans* (1920).

The doctrine of waiver has never been fully developed by the courts and aspects of it remain uncertain, but it is clearly closely akin to the equitable doctrine of promissory estoppel (see Chapter 4).

PERFORMANCE

If both parties perform their obligations under the contract, the contract is discharged. This raises the question, what amounts to performance?

The general rule is that performance must be precise and exact. Thus, in one case, the defendants agreed to buy from the claimants 3,000 tins of canned fruit to be packed in cases containing 30 tins. Some of the consignment was packed in cases containing 24 tins and it was held that the defendants were entitled to reject the whole consignment; *Re Moore Co* and *Landauer Co* (1921) (criticised in *Reardon Smith Line Ltd v Hansen-Tangen*, HL, 1976). It should be noted, however, that in non-consumer sales, s.15A of the Sale of Goods Act 1979 (as inserted by s.4(1) of the Sale and Supply of Goods Act 1994) prevents the purchaser from unreasonably rejecting goods which are only slightly different from the contract description, subject to any contrary provisions in the contract. The hardship of the rule is illustrated by *Cutter v Powell* (1795), where a seaman, having agreed to serve on a ship from Jamaica to Liverpool for 30 guineas payable on completion of the voyage, died in mid-voyage. The contract was construed to be "entire" and therefore his widow could recover nothing in respect of the work done.

The hardship of the general rule is mitigated by various exceptions:

Severable contracts

"Entire" contracts tend to be the exception rather than the rule. A contract will be "severable" where some of the obligations in the contract may be enforced independently of performance by the other party.

Whether obligations are entire or severable is a question of construction; the tendency in contracts for work and materials is towards severability. Thus, in *Roberts v Havelock* (1832), a ship en route was damaged and had to be docked for essential repairs. The claimant carried out the repairs, but before he had completed the contract, he requested payment for work carried out thus far. His action succeeded as the contract did not require him to complete all the repairs before he made a demand for payment.

Substantial performance

A party who performs his contractual obligations substantially though not precisely, may enforce the contract; *Boone v Eyre* (1779). However, the substantial performer may himself be liable for damages in respect of his partial performance. Two cases illustrate the operation of the doctrine.

In *H. Dakin Co Ltd v Lee*, CA, 1916, the claimant builders agreed to carry out repairs to the defendant's house. The work as carried out departed from the specification in three minor respects which could be remedied at a relatively small cost. The Court of Appeal gave judgment for the claimant, subject to a deduction equal to the cost of remedying the defects.

In *Bolton v Mahadeva*, CA, 1972, the claimant agreed to install central heating in the defendant's house for £560. The system was defective in that the house was not heated adequately and noxious fumes were given off inside the house. The cost of remedying the defects was £174. The Court of Appeal held that there had not been substantial performance and the claimant was not entitled to recover anything.

In order to rely on the doctrine of substantial performance, the claimant's breach must amount only to a breach of warranty, or a non-serious breach of an innominate term. Where they have broken a condition, they cannot rely on the doctrine.

Voluntary acceptance of partial performance

Where performance by one party is only partial, the other party may accept the partial performance; *Christy v Row* (1808). Implicit in the idea of acceptance of partial performance is the notion that the parties have effectively entered into a fresh agreement.

Where partial performance is accepted, the partial performer will have a claim on a *quantum meruit* basis in respect of work done (see Chapter 14).

The other party must have a genuine choice whether or not to accept the partial performance. In *Sumpter v Hedges*, CA, 1898, the claimant agreed to erect buildings on the defendant's land. He did about two-thirds of the work and then abandoned the contract, leaving the defendant himself to complete the buildings. The claimant's action on *quantum meruit* failed; the defendant had no choice whether to accept or reject the partial performance.

Prevention of performance by breach or frustration

A party may be wrongfully prevented by the other party from completing performance. The injured party in such a situation may claim damages for breach of contract or claim on a *quantum meruit* for the work done; *Planché v Colburn* (1831).

Alternatively, if the contract is frustrated, it is automatically discharged and the parties excused further performance.

TENDER OF PERFORMANCE

Where one party is unable to complete performance without the collaboration of the other party, they may make an offer or "tender" of performance which is rejected by the other party. If this is the case, the party tendering performance will be discharged from further liability. Thus, a tender of performance is equivalent to performance.

In *Startup v Macdonald* (1843), the claimant, having agreed to deliver oil within the last 14 days of March, tried to deliver it at 8.30 p.m. on the last day of that month, but the defendant refused to take delivery. The claimant's action for damages succeeded.

However, s.29(5) of the Sale of Goods Act 1979 enacts that a tender of goods must be made at a reasonable hour; what is reasonable is a question of fact.

Where a party is under a contractual obligation to pay a sum of money, a tender of money by that party, if refused by the other party, will not discharge the tenderer from liability. If sued, the tenderer may pay the sum of money into court and if the action is proceeded with, the other party may be ordered to pay costs.

STIPULATIONS AS TO TIME

Where the contract does not fix a time for performance, as a general rule performance must be effected within a reasonable time. This is given statutory effect by s.29(3) of the Sale of Goods Act 1979 in relation to the obligation to deliver the goods under a contract of sale.

At common law, where a time was fixed for performance of one party's obligations under the contract, time was "of the essence". The failure to perform by the appointed date amounted to a breach of contract entitling the innocent party to treat themselves as discharged. Nevertheless, equity would grant specific performance despite a failure to comply with a stipulation as to time, and s.41 of the Law of Property Act 1925 (re-enacting s.25 of the Judicature Act 1873) provides that the equitable principle shall prevail.

The result is that time is not of the essence where a contract fixes a date for performance unless it falls under one of the following exceptional cases:

(1) where the contract expressly provides that time is of the essence;

(2) where the contract was not originally one where time was of the essence, but it is made of the essence by a party subjected to unreasonable delay giving notice to the other party to perform within a reasonable time;

(3) where it must be inferred from the nature of the subject-matter and the circumstances surrounding the contract that time is of the essence.

Where time is of the essence in a contract, it is clear that any delay, however slight, will amount to repudiation; *Union Eagle Ltd v Golden Achievement Ltd*, PC, 1997.

Where time is not of the essence, the failure to perform by the stipulated time is still nevertheless a breach of contract entitling the injured party to damages; *Raineri v Miles*, HL, 1980.

---

14. REMEDIES

Where a party to a contract suffers loss as a result of a breach they will be entitled to an award of damages. Alternatively, they may bring a claim on a *quantum meruit* for the benefit of work partially completed under the contract. In an appropriate case, the court may exercise its equitable jurisdiction to grant an order of specific performance or an injunction.

These remedies will be considered below.

DAMAGES

Basis of the award

Damages are normally awarded on the basis of placing the injured party in the same financial position as if the contract had been properly performed, i.e. compensation for "loss of bargain" or loss of expectations under the contract.

Exceptionally, damages are awarded to compensate the claimant for expenses incurred in reliance on the contract which have been wasted by the defendant's breach. The object of damages for reliance loss is to place the claimant in the position they would have been in had the contract never been made.

Where damages are awarded on the reliance basis, it seems that pre-contractual expenses may be included. In *Anglia Television Ltd v Reed*, CA, 1971, the claimants engaged the defendant, an actor, to play a part in a film. Before this, the claimants had incurred expenditure in employing a director and a designer. The defendant repudiated the contract and it was held that the claimants were entitled to recover their wasted expenditure. However, in *C. and P. Haulage v Middleton*, CA, 1983, the Court of Appeal awarded only nominal damages on the reliance basis as the bargain the claimant had entered into turned out to be a bad one for him; i.e. the expenditure was not wasted by the defendant's breach.

In the *Anglia Television* case (above), it seems to have been assumed that the film, if made, would have made enough money to at least cover the claimant's expenditure. In *C.C.C. Films (London) Ltd v Impact Quadrant Films Ltd* (1984), a case not dissimilar on the facts, it was held that the burden lay on the defendant to show that the transaction was so unprofitable as to not even cover the claimant's expenses.

It seems that in a suitable case, damages can be measured by the benefit gained by the wrongdoer from the breach; *Wrotham Park Estate Co Ltd v Parkside Homes Ltd* (1974). This principle was applied in unusual circumstances in *Attorney-General v Blake*, HL, 2000. Blake, a British intelligence officer, had spied for the Soviet Union and was convicted and imprisoned for treason. He escaped and defected to Moscow where he wrote an autobiography which was published in England. Publication was a breach of Blake's former contract of employment. An injunction was granted preventing payment of the royalties to Blake.

There are, however, limits to the application of the above-stated principle. In *Experience Hendrix v PPX Enterprises*, CA, 2003, an action was brought to compel a company who had released some unlicensed recordings of guitarist Jimi Hendrix's music to provide a full account of profits. The Court of Appeal held that the case was not sufficiently exceptional in that, unlike Blake, it did not involve national security nor was there any element of a fiduciary obligation. The Court held that the defendants should pay the claimants merely a reasonable sum for their use of the recordings.

Contributory negligence

Although it is clear that contractual liability may be removed altogether by the claimant's fault (*Quinn v Burch Bros (Builders) Ltd* (1966)), the law has been less clear whether damages for breach of contract can be apportioned by the court on the ground of the claimant's contributory negligence under the Law Reform (Contributory Negligence) Act 1945.

The law has now been clarified as a result of *Forsikringsaktieselskapet Vesta v Butcher*, CA, 1988. Where the defendant's liability in contract is the same as his liability in the tort of negligence independently of the existence of any contract, the defendant may raise the defence of contributory negligence whether the action is brought in contract or tort. However, where contractual liability is strict the Act of 1945 does not apply; *Barclays Bank v Fairclough Building Ltd*, CA, 1994.

Damages for mental distress

Although damages in contract may be recovered for physical inconvenience and pain and suffering caused by personal injury, it was always thought that damages could not generally be recovered for mental distress; *Addis v Gramophone Co Ltd*, HL, 1909. Here, the House of Lords refused to award damages for injury to feelings in a wrongful dismissal case. However, where the mental distress results from an employer's breach of an implied term concerning trust and confidence, there is no reason in principle why such damages should not be awarded; *Johnson v Unisys Ltd*, HL, 2001. Where the contract is for a holiday, recreation or entertainment, it is clear that substantial damages may be recoverable for disappointment, vexation and mental distress; *Jarvis v Swann Tours*, CA, 1973. Damages may also be awarded for loss of reputation; so-called "stigma compensation". Thus, in *Malik v Bank of Credit and Commerce International SA (in compulsory liquidation)*, HL, 1998, the House of Lords held that employees could recover damages for financial loss caused by difficulty in obtaining alternative employment, on the basis that the employer had breached an implied term not to conduct its business dishonestly. It was therefore reasonably foreseeable that the breach would harm the claimants' employment prospects in future.

Despite some earlier cases which seemed to call into question the *Addis* principle, it now seems to have been confirmed, at least in relation to contracts of employment; *Bliss v South East Thames Regional Health Authority*, CA, 1985. A similar approach was taken by the Court of Appeal in relation to a contract to buy a house in *Watts v Morrow*, CA, 1991. This case was distinguished in *Farley v Skinner* (No.2), HL, 2001 where a home-buyer employed a surveyor to investigate whether a country house was affected by aircraft noise. It was held that the claimant was entitled, in principle, to recover non-pecuniary damages for distress and inconvenience resulting from the surveyor's negligence. The House of Lords considered that, in future, it will be "sufficient if a major or important object of the contract is to give pleasure, relaxation or piece of mind". However, the damages awarded by the courts under this head should be modest—in *Farley v Skinner* the sum of £10, 000 was awarded.

Remoteness of damage

The claimant may not be able to recover damages for all the loss they have suffered as some of the loss may be adjudged by the court to be too remote a consequence of the breach to be compensatable by the defendant.

The rules concerning remoteness of damage were originally laid down in *Hadley v Baxendale* (1854). Here, the claimants were millers who contracted with the defendant carriers to take a broken mill shaft to the repairers, as a pattern for a new shaft. The claimants had no spare shaft. Although the defendants had promised to deliver within a day, they in fact delayed, and the shaft was not delivered until a week later. The claimants sued the defendants for damages for loss of profits arising from the fact that the mill was out of action for longer than anticipated, owing to the delay.

Alderson B. said that damages for breach of contract "should be such as may fairly and reasonably be considered either arising naturally, i.e. according to the usual course of things, from such breach of contract itself, or such as may reasonably be supposed to have been in the contemplation of both parties, at the time they made the contract, as the probable result of the breach of it."

Applying the above, the court held that the defendants were not liable for the loss of profits. The claimant's loss did not arise "naturally" because the claimants might well have possessed a spare shaft; neither was it "in the contemplation of the parties", as the defendants were unaware that the shaft entrusted to them was the only one which the claimants possessed. Accordingly, loss of profits was too remote a head of damages.

The principle laid down in *Hadley v Baxendale* was restated by the Court of Appeal in *Victoria Laundry (Windsor) Ltd v Newman Industries Ltd*, CA, 1949 and discussed by the House of Lords in *The Heron II*, HL, 1969. As a result of these cases, remoteness of damage may be divided into two sub-rules (below), one of which must be satisfied if a particular head of damage is not to be adjudged too remote. Thus, the claimant may recover for:

(1) loss arising naturally out of the breach, i.e. in the ordinary course of things. As a reasonable person, the contract-breaking party is taken to know what this loss will be; or

(2) (in relation to special, abnormal or unusual loss) loss which could reasonably be supposed to have been within the contemplation of the parties, at the time of the contract, as the probable result of the breach.

Further, the courts have held that provided a particular type of loss is within the reasonable contemplation of the parties, the loss will not be too remote if its extent was far more serious than could have been reasonably contemplated; *H. Parsons (Livestock) Ltd v Uttley Ingham Co Ltd*, CA, 1978; *Brown v K M R Services Ltd*, CA, 1995.

A classic illustration of the workings of the remoteness rules is afforded by the *Victoria Laundry* case. The claimants, launderers and dyers, wished to acquire another boiler to enable them to expand their business and to take on certain lucrative dyeing contracts. The defendants agreed to sell to the claimants a boiler which, as the defendants were aware, was required for immediate use. Delivery was five months late and the claimants claimed loss of profits as follows:

(1) £16 per week representing loss of "normal" profits representing the additional custom they would have taken on; and

(2) £262 per week representing the loss of the lucrative dyeing contracts.

The Court of Appeal held that the defendants' state of knowledge made them liable for (1), but not (2), about which they neither knew nor could be taken to know. A similar approach was taken in *Balfour Beatty Construction (Scotland) Ltd v Scottish Power Plc*, HL, 1994 where it was held that there was no general principle that parties were presumed to have knowledge of each other's business practices, especially where complex construction or manufacturing processes were involved.

The case of *Kemp v Intasun Holidays*, CA, 1987 affords an interesting comparison. A holiday-maker verbally informed his travel agent that he was prone to asthma attacks. Whilst on holiday, the defendants, in breach of contract, required the claimant to relocate his hotel accommodation which triggered off an asthma attack. On a claim for additional damages, the court held that the mention of asthma was merely conversational and not part of the booking as the claimant had left blank a box on the booking form headed "Special Requests". Sub-rule (ii) in *Hadley v Baxendale* did not therefore come into play.

Measure of damages

Once it is established that loss is not too remote, the next question is the measure of damages, i.e. how is the loss to be quantified?

There are no specific rules for the quantification of damages in contract; quantification is a matter for the court. One exception concerns contracts for the sale of goods. Section 51 of the Sale of Goods Act 1979 provides that where the seller fails to deliver the goods and the buyer brings an action for non-delivery, where there is an available market for the goods, the measure of damages should be the difference between the contract price and the current market price at the time when the goods ought to have been delivered.

Similarly, where the buyer refuses to accept or pay for the goods, s.50 provides that where there is an available market, the measure of damages should be the difference between the contract price and the current market price at the time when the goods ought to have been accepted. Where the seller is a dealer, the loss arising in the usual course of things is the loss of profit that would have been made had the goods been sold to that particular buyer. If they have been able to find another buyer at the same or higher price, their damages will be nominal; *Charter v Sullivan*, CA, 1957. Where supply exceeds demand, full loss of profit may be awarded as the dealer will have sold one less item than they otherwise would; *W.L. Thompson Ltd v Robinson (Gunmakers) Ltd* (1955).

In any type of contract, the fact that an award of damages involves an element of speculation will not prevent the award being made. In *Chaplin v Hicks*, CA, 1911, the claimant recovered substantial damages against the organiser of a beauty competition, who had failed, in breach of contract, to invite her for interview. The Court of Appeal refused to upset the award even though the claimant was by no means certain to have been successful.

It seems that in building contracts, there are two principal measures of damages, (i) difference in value; and (ii) cost of reinstatement. In *Ruxley Electronics and Construction Ltd v Forsyth*, HL, 1995, their Lordships held that where it would be unreasonable to award the cost of reinstatement the court should award the difference in value. An example is where the expense of reinstatement would be out of proportion to the benefit to be obtained. In *Ruxley*, the defendant contracted for the construction of a swimming pool of a maximum depth of 7ft. 6in., but on completion the pool was only 6ft. 9in. deep. As the pool was perfectly serviceable it was held that the appropriate measure was the difference in value. This difference was nil although the trial judge's award of £2,500 for loss of amenity was upheld. The cost of reconstruction would have amounted to over £20,000.

Mitigation

There is a duty on the claimant to take all reasonable steps to mitigate the loss caused by the breach of contract.

Recovery cannot be made for any part of the loss which the defendant can prove to have resulted from a failure to mitigate; *British Westinghouse Electric Co v Underground Electric Railway Co of London*, HL, 1912.

In *Brace v Calder* (1895) the defendants were a four-member partnership who agreed to employ the claimant as manager for two years. Shortly after, the partnership was dissolved which amounted to wrongful dismissal of the claimant. Then two of the former partners offered to employ the claimant on the same terms but he refused the offer. The claimant brought an action to recover the salary he would have received had he served the full two years. It was held that he was entitled only to nominal damages as it was unreasonable to have rejected the offer of continued employment.

The claimant is only required to act reasonably; they would not be required, in order to mitigate, to embark on a hazardous or uncertain course of action; *Pilkington v Wood* (1953). Further, if, on an anticipatory breach (see Chapter 13), the injured party elects to affirm the contract instead of accepting the repudiation, they will be under no duty to mitigate before the date due for performance.

Liquidated damages and penalties

A contract may contain a clause providing for the payment of a fixed sum on breach. If the sum represents a genuine pre-estimate of the loss, the court will allow the claimant, on breach, to recover this sum without proof of actual loss. This is so whether the actual loss is greater or smaller than the sum stipulated in the contract. Such provisions are usually referred to as "liquidated damages" or "agreed damages" clauses.

Where the sum stipulated in the contract is not a genuine pre-estimate of the loss, but is more in the nature of a threat held over the head of the other party to compel performance, it is referred to as a "penalty". A penalty is invalid and a claimant who attempts to enforce a penalty may recover compensation only for their actual loss.

In the unlikely event that the loss exceeds the sum stipulated in the penalty clause, the claimant may elect to recover his or her full loss; this option does not exist in the case of liquidated damages. Whether a clause is a liquidated damages clause or a penalty is a question of construction depending upon the intention of the parties judged as at the time the contract was made. The following rules for the guidance of the court were laid down in *Dunlop Pneumatic Tyre Co Ltd v New Garage and Motor Co Ltd*, HL, 1915:

(1) The expression used by the parties to describe the sum is a relevant, but not a conclusive, factor; e.g. it may be described as "agreed damages" but in fact be a penalty, and vice versa.

(2) If the sum stipulated for is extravagant and unconscionable in relation to the greatest loss which could conceivably follow the breach, it will be a penalty.

(3) Where the breach consists of the non-payment of a sum of money and the sum to be paid on breach is greater than the sum which ought to have been paid, the sum is a penalty.

(4) There is a presumption (but no more) that where a single lump sum is to be paid on the occurrence of one or more or all of several events, some serious and others not, the lump sum is a penalty.

(5) A sum is not prevented from being liquidated damages by the fact that precise pre-estimation of the loss is impossible.

In the *Dunlop* case itself, the claimants supplied tyres to the defendants subject to an agreement that the defendants would not, inter alia, resell them below list price. The defendants had to pay £5 "by way of liquidated damages and not as a penalty" for every tyre sold in breach of the agreement. The House of Lords held that this provision was not penal and was in the nature of liquidated damages. Undercutting would certainly have damaged the claimants' business, and though precise pre-estimation estimation of the loss was impossible, the sum stipulated for here was reasonable in the circumstances.

Sometimes a contract may stipulate for a sum of money to be paid upon the occurrence of an event that is not a breach of contract, as in *Adler v Moore* (1961). The House of Lords have confirmed, in *Export Credit Guarantee Department v Universal Oil*

Products Co, HL, 1983 that the penalty rules (set out above) only apply to sums of money payable on breach. But, in *Jobson v Johnson*, CA, 1988 the court held that the equitable rules against contractual penalty clauses applied where the penalty involved the transfer of property whose value exceeded the actual loss of the innocent party, as well as where it involved the payment of an excessive sum of money.

ACTION FOR AN AGREED SUM

An action for damages in contract as discussed above must be distinguished from an action for an agreed sum, such as an agreed price for work and materials or the price of goods sold. In an action for an agreed sum, the issues of remoteness and measures of damages (as discussed above) do not arise, although the action will not be available if damages are in fact an adequate remedy. There is, however, an exception to this last point; i.e. where the situation in *White and Carter (Councils) Ltd v McGregor*, HL, 1962, applies. Here, the appellants agreed to advertise the respondents' business on litter-bins for a period of three years at an agreed price. The respondents repudiated the contract the very day it was made but the appellants chose to ignore the repudiation and displayed the advertisements for three years, eventually claiming the full amount due under the contract. The majority of the House of Lords held that the appellants were entitled to recover the amount agreed under the contract.

There has been some controversy concerning this decision and it is subject to certain limitations:

(1) it will not apply where the co-operation of the other party is required, such as where work under the contract is carried out on the defendant's land, as in *Hounslow L.P.C. v Twickenham Garden Developments Ltd* (1971); and

(2) it may not apply where the claimant has no legitimate financial or other interest in performing the contract rather than claiming damages, such as business commitments with third parties. The legitimate interest factor was allowed in *The Odenfeld* (1978) and rejected in *Clea Shipping Corp v Bulk Oil International Ltd* (1984). A possible further limitation is suggested by *Attica Sea Carriers Corp v Ferrostaal Poseidon Buld Reederei GmbH*, CA, 1976 where Lord Denning M.R. was of the view that a party cannot

rely on the *White and Carter* principle where they ought in all reason to accept the other party's repudiation and sue for damages immediately.

QUANTUM MERUIT

A claim on a *quantum meruit*; ("as much as he deserves") is a claim for reasonable remuneration. The remedy is distinct from an award of damages which is essentially compensation for loss. A claim on a *quantum meruit* may arise where one party is prevented by the other (in breach), from completing performance. The injured party may claim on a *quantum meruit*; *Planche v Colburn* (1831). In this situation, the remedy is available as an alternative to claiming damages. Similarly, a claim may arise where a partial performance is voluntarily accepted by the other party; the partial performer may sue on a (see under "Discharge by Performance," Chapter 13).

SPECIFIC PERFORMANCE AND INJUNCTION

Specific performance and injunction are equitable remedies, not available as of right but at the discretion of the court (cf. damages). The remedies will only be granted where it is equitable to do so, and may be refused on the ground of hardship.

Specific performance

Specific performance is an order of the court compelling the defendant to perform their part of the contract. The court has power to award damages in addition to, or instead of, specific performance. The fact that the remedy may be refused on the ground of hardship is illustrated by *Patel v Ali* (1984). Specific performance was refused of a contract for the sale of a house, as the defendant vendor, who spoke little English, had contracted a serious illness and needed to be near friends and relatives. The claimant was left to the common law remedy of damages on the ground that exceptional hardship would result if specific performance was granted.

The remedy is subject to certain limitations:

(1) Damages inadequate: Specific performance will only be granted where damages are an inadequate remedy. Thus, it will not, in general, be awarded of a contract for the sale

of goods (*Cohen v Roche* (1927)), although the power to award it is contained in s.52 of the Sale of Goods Act 1979.

Specific performance is most commonly ordered in relation to the breach of contract for the sale of land, since, land being unique, damages will not usually be adequate compensation. In *Beswick v Beswick*, HL, 1968, the remedy was granted to enforce a contractual obligation to pay a sum of money (see Chapter 12).

(2) Contracts requiring constant supervision: Specific performance will not be granted where the constant supervision of the court would be required, e.g. where a contract required a resident porter to be in attendance at a block of flats, the remedy was refused; *Ryan v Mutual Tontine Westminster Chambers Association*, CA, 1893. The principle was applied to a covenant in a commercial lease in *Co-operative Insurance Ltd v Argyll Stores (Holdings) Ltd*, HL, 1997.

(3) Contracts for personal services: Specific performance will not be awarded where the contract involves personal services, e.g. a contract of employment.

(4) Lack of mutuality: Specific performance will not, in general, be ordered against a defendant unless the remedy could have been ordered against the plaintiff, e.g. a plaintiff who is a minor; *Flight v Bolland* (1828). Mutuality is normally considered as at the time of the judgment rather than the time when the contract was made; *Price v Strange*, CA, 1977.

Injunction

An injunction may be granted to restrain a breach of negative stipulation (a promise not to do something) in a contract.

There is a general principle that an injunction will not be granted if its effect would be to compel a party to a contract to do something which could not have been made subject to an order of specific performance, e.g. to require performance of a contract for personal services. In *Page One Records Ltd v Britton* (1968), the manager of the pop group The Troggs sought an injunction restraining them from appointing, in breach of contract, anyone else as manager. The injunction was refused on the ground that, if granted, its effect would be to compel performance of a personal services contract. Very exceptionally an injunction may be granted in these circumstances, for example, where an employee is dismissed in breach of contract as a result of trade union pressure; *Hill v CA Parsons Co Ltd*, CA, 1972.

An injunction may be granted to restrain a breach of a negative stipulation in a personal services contract providing it does not actually compel performance. In *Warner Bros Pictures Inc. v Nelson* (1937), the actress Bette Davis agreed with the plaintiffs not to act for any other film company for a year; during that period she did work for another company. An injunction was granted restraining her from so doing; the effect of the injunction was to encourage, rather than compel, performance since she would be free to earn her living in some way other than acting.

OTHER REMEDIES

In addition to the remedies discussed in this chapter, the following should be noted. Where there is a serious breach of contract, the innocent party may elect to treat their self as discharged from the contract in addition to claiming damages (see Chapter 6). The remedy of rescission exists where a misrepresentation has induced the contract (Chapter 8) and in the case of duress or undue influence (Chapter 10). The remedy of rectification is discussed in Chapter 9.

LIMITATION OF ACTIONS

The right to bring proceedings in respect of a breach of contract may be extinguished by the passage of time under the Limitation Act 1980.

Where the action is founded upon a simple contract, the period of limitation (after which proceedings are barred) is six years from the date on which the cause of action accrued (s.5).

Where the claimant seeks damages for personal injuries arising out of a breach of contract, the normal period of limitation is three years (s.11).

Where the action is founded upon a contract by deed, the period of limitation is 12 years (s.8). Where fraud and mistake are involved, the period of limitation does not begin to run until the claimant has discovered the fraud or mistake or with reasonable diligence could have discovered it (s.32).

Where the claimant is under a disability, e.g. a person of unsound mind, time begins to run from the date that disability ceases or the claimant dies, whichever is the first (ss.28 and 38).

The period of limitation may be extended if the defendant acknowledges the claim or makes some payment in respect of it.

If this is the case, time will begin to run once more from the date of the acknowledgement or part-payment (s.29).

15. EXAMINATION CHECKLIST

(1) Have the parties, viewed objectively, reached agreement? Is there an offer, or is it merely an invitation to treat?

(2) Has the offer been unequivocally accepted? Or has the offeree made a counter-offer? Alternatively, has the offer been revoked or has it lapsed?

(3) Note the effect of acceptances by post where the postal rule applies. Compare the position of revocations, which must be communicated.

(4) Has the promise been supported by consideration? Or is the consideration "past"? Is it insufficient because it consists of the performance of:

    (a) an existing public duty; or

    (b) an existing contractual duty (however note the effect of the decision in *Williams v Roffey* here)?

Remember the rule about existing contractual duty owed to a third party in *Shadwell v Shadwell*.

(5) If the part payment of a debt is involved, note that this will not constitute consideration unless;

    (a) one of the three exceptions in *Pinnel's* Case applies;

    (b) it involves part payment by a third party;

    (c) there is a composition agreement with creditors.

(6) Even in the absence of consideration, does the principle of promissory estoppel apply? Note the requirements which must be satisfied before the doctrine comes into play;

    (a) a clear and unequivocal promise by the promisor not to insist on strict legal rights;

    (b) action in reliance by the promisee;

    (c) it must be inequitable for the promisor to revert to strict legal rights;

    (d) the doctrine may only be raised as a defence.

(7) Are any statements made representations or terms? Apply the guidelines:

    (a) manner and timing of statement;

   (b) importance of statement;
   (c) special knowledge and skill on the part of the maker of the statement;
   (d) has it been reduced to writing?

(8) If the statement is a term, is it:

   (a) a condition;
   (b) a warranty;
   (c) an innominate term?

Note the practical effect of the above distinction in terms of the remedies available to the innocent party.
(9) Have any terms been implied into the contract by custom, statute or the courts?
(10) If it is a sale of goods transaction, what terms will be implied?
(11) If there is a clause of exclusion or limitation, has it been incorporated into the contract? Such terms may be incorporated by signature, notice or previous dealings.
(12) Remember that exclusion clauses will be construed contra proferentem although the rule is applied less strictly to limitation clauses.
(13) Apply the provisions of the Unfair Contract Terms Act 1977. Is the claimant a consumer as defined by the Act? Note the applicability of the following sections of the Act;

   (a) sale of goods and hire purchase (s.6);
   (b) supply of goods and services (s.7);
   (c) negligence liability (s.2);
   (d) liability for breach of contract (s.3).

(14) Where the reasonableness test in s.11 applies, what factors are relevant? See the guidelines in Sch. 2 to the Act and the criteria of Lord Bridge in *George Mitchell (Chesterhall) Ltd v Finney Lock Seeds Ltd.*
(15) Do the Unfair Terms in Consumer Contracts Regulations 1999 apply?

   (a) is the claimant a consumer as defined by the Regulations?
   (b) Is the contract one between a seller/supplier and consumer where the term in question has not been individually negotiated?

   (c) The Regulations will not apply to a core provision or one concerning the adequacy of the price.

   (d) If the Regulations apply to a term, it will not be binding if it is unfair.

(16) Has the transaction been induced by an actionable misrepresentation? If so, it will be voidable.

(17) Actionable misrepresentation consists of a false statement of fact which induces the other party to enter the contract; note that statements of intention, opinion and law are excluded unless dishonest; *Edgington v Fitzmaurice*. What is mean by "inducement" in this context?

(18) Remember the rule about silence not being misrepresentation and the exceptions to it.

(19) You must be able to distinguish between fraudulent, negligent and innocent misrepresentation and the consequences of each. What remedies are available at common law, in equity and under the Misrepresentation Act 1967?

(20) When will the right to rescind a contract for misrepresentation be lost?

(21) What is the distinction between a common, mutual and unilateral mistake? When will such mistakes be operative?

(22) How is a common mistake as to quality dealt with at common law?

(23) When will a unilateral mistake as to identity be operative?

(24) Distinguish between duress and undue influence. Note the distinction between actual and presumed undue influence. Where the undue influence (or other legal wrong) may have been applied by a third party, note the guidelines laid down in *Royal Bank of Scotland Plc v Etridge (No.2)*.

(25) Which contracts fall within the restraint of trade doctrine? What are the two traditional proprietary interests that merit protection here?

(26) Remember that a covenant in restraint of trade will be void if wider than reasonably necessary to protect the relevant interest. However, this is subject to (a) "flexible" construction; and (b) the doctrine of severance.

(27) What are the four ways in which a contract may be discharged?

(28) When will a contract be frustrated? What are examples of impossibility, illegality or radical change in the circumstances?

(29) Note the effect at common law of frustration and how this was affected by the Law Reform (Frustrated Contracts) Act 1943. Remember that;

(a) Section 1(2) deals with the recovery of money paid; and
(b) Section 1(3) deals with valuable benefit.

(30) What are the exceptions to the rule about precise performance?
(31) Ensure that you are familiar with the rule of remoteness of damage in *Hadley v Baxendale*. Note the different treatment of;

(a) normal loss; and
(b) special, abnormal or unusual loss.

(32) When will the claimant be under a duty to mitigate the loss in a claim for damages?
(33) Make sure you understand the difference between "penalty" and "liquidated damages". What guidelines have been laid down in order to distinguish between them?
(34) What are the limitations, in the law of contract, upon the grant of injunctions and decrees of specific performance?

16. SAMPLE QUESTIONS AND MODEL ANSWERS

Question 1

XYZ Co, who manufacture oil rigs, wrote to Mogul Ltd, an oil company, offering to construct an oil rig for £1,000,000. The offer was made on a form containing XYZ's standard terms of business. One of the terms contained in the document was that the initially agreed contract price might be varied according to the cost and availability of materials.

Mogul replied, in a letter containing their standard terms of business, stating that they wished to order the rig. These terms did not include a price variation clause but contained a statement that the order was not valid unless confirmed by return of post. XYZ duly confirmed by a letter dated May 1 which was delayed in the post as it bore the wrong address and did not arrive until May 14. Meanwhile, on May 12, Mogul posted a letter to XYZ cancelling the order which arrived on May 13. XYZ ignored this letter and pressed on with the construction of the rig. It was completed one year later at a price of £2,000,000. Mogul refuse to take delivery. Advise Mogul Ltd.

Answer

Whether or not Mogul can refuse to take delivery depends upon whether or not there is a binding contract between XYZ and Mogul. XYZ made the initial offer on their standard terms of business. As Mogul's reply is on different terms, it would seem to be in the nature of a counter-offer, rather than an acceptance. It was held in *Hyde v Wrench* (1840) that the effect of a counter-offer is to operate as a rejection of the original offer. However, the counter-offer is itself an offer and may be accepted on its own terms.

The problem here is often referred to as the "battle of the forms". Although it has been argued that, in this situation, the contract should be concluded on the original offeror's terms as the offeree, by purporting to accept, waives his own terms, the Court of Appeal in *Butler Machine Tool Co Ltd v Ex-Cell-O Corp*, CA, 1979 preferred to adopt the traditional view that the offeree in such a situation makes a counter-offer.

The next question is whether Mogul's counter-offer has been accepted by XYZ. The general rule is that acceptance must be communicated. If XYZ's letter of confirmation was only effective when communicated, i.e. when it arrived on May 14, there would be no contract because the counter-offer would have been revoked by Mogul's letter of cancellation which arrived on May 13. Revocation is effective when communicated; *Byrne Co v Van Tienhoven Co* (1880). However, where the post is the proper means of communication between the parties, a letter of acceptance is effective immediately it is posted even if delayed or lost; *Household Fire, etc., Insurance Co v Grant* (1879). If the postal rule of acceptance were to apply here, the contract would be concluded on the date of posting which we may take to be May 1 and Mogul's purported revocation would be ineffective.

On the facts, there is reason to question whether the postal rule of acceptance would apply. First, it is possible to argue that the wording of the counter-offer ("confirm by return of post") might be construed as requiring actual communication to arrive within a short period. In *Holwell Securities Ltd v Hughes*, CA, 1974, an offer to sell land stipulated that acceptance should be "by notice in writing". It was held that the form of the words excluded the postal rule of acceptance. In this case, everything would depend upon the interpretation placed by the court on the words used. Secondly, the letter of acceptance was delayed because it was misaddressed. Although there is no authority directly on the point, it is thought that if the misdirection is due to the offeree's carelessness, the postal rule of acceptance will not apply. This is suggested by the analogous case of *Getreide-Import Gesellschaft v Contimar* (1953). Nevertheless, the misdirection could be the fault of the offeror, e.g. in supplying the wrong address. In such a case, *Treitel* (Law of Contract, 6th ed.) has suggested that the true rule is that a misdirected acceptance takes effect (if at all) at the time which is least favourable to the party responsible for misdirection. In this case, if the fault were traceable to Mogul, the postal rule of acceptance might be held to apply.

If the contract is binding due to a valid postal acceptance, Mogul's letter of May 12 could be regarded as a repudiatory breach of contract. XYZ are not bound to accept the repudiation and in the circumstances are under no duty to mitigate. On the authority of *White and Carter (Councils) Ltd v McGregor*, HL, 1961, XYZ would be entitled to complete performance and claim the contractual sum due, which would presumably be £1,000,000 as the price variation clause is excluded from the contract. However, this principle is subject to the limitation that it will not apply where the plaintiff has no substantial or legitimate interest in completing performance rather than claiming damages (per Lord Reid in *White and Carter*.) It is conceivable that a manufacturer of large capital goods could have such an interest, though the position may ultimately depend on whether XYZ have acted wholly unreasonably in completing performance rather than claiming damages; *Attica Sea Carriers* Case (CA, 1976).

It would seem that Mogül's best hope is to show that no contract was concluded.

Question 2

Robin is the owner of the Maid Marion Hotel in Nottingley. He wanted to attract more custom to the hotel and so decided to build an indoor swimming pool. He approached the Sheriff Bank to arrange suitable finance for the project.

In March, the Sheriff Bank agreed to loan £120,000 to Robin to be repaid in 12 monthly instalments of £10,000 each plus agreed interest.

Robin contracted with Oak Tree Developments Ltd (OTD) for the pool to be fully constructed and completed by December 1. The noise and disruption caused by the construction meant that hotel bookings were reduced and Robin was soon in financial difficulties. He managed to repay the first six instalments as they fell due but then asked the Sheriff Bank if they would write off the remainder of the debt. This was reluctantly agreed to.

OTD then informed Robin that they might have some difficulty in completing the pool by December 1. Robin promised OTD a bonus of £2,500 if they would "pull out all the stops" and complete the pool on time. Robin also promised every employee of OTD a bonus of £50 each if they got the job done on time.

The pool was in fact completed on time and the hotel attracted a lot of new custom. However, the Sheriff Bank is now demanding that Robin pay the remaining instalments due in respect of the loan as well as all of the arrears. Robin is now refusing to pay any bonuses to either OTD or their employees.

Discuss the legal position.

Answer

Sheriff Bank—the bank has made a promise not to insist on its strict legal rights. At common law, such promises must be supported by consideration. It was established in *Pinnel's* case, and confirmed by the *House of Lords in Foakes v Beer*, HL, 1884, that part payment of a debt is not good consideration for a promise to forgo the balance. On this basis the promise of the bank is not binding as Robin has furnished no additional consideration other than that he was originally bound to do.

Although it was held in *Williams v Roffey Bros*, CA, 1990 that the performance of an existing contractual duty can amount to good consideration if a practical benefit is conferred on the promisor, the Court of Appeal in *Re Selectmove*, CA, 1995 held that the principle in *Williams v Roffey* cannot be extended to debtor-creditor relationships. It seems it must be confined to obligations to supply goods and services—to hold otherwise would undermine the authority of *Foakes v Beer*. Nevertheless, Robin may be able to rely on the doctrine of promissory estoppel. The doctrine was originally enunciated by Lord Cairns L.C. *in Hughes v Metropolitan Railway Co*, HL, 1877 and adopted by Denning J, *obiter*, in *Central London Property Trust Ltd v High Trees House Ltd*, 1947 who stated that: "the logical consequence [of the doctrine] is that a promise to accept a smaller sum in discharge of a larger sum, if acted upon, is binding notwithstanding the absence of consideration".

The effect of the doctrine is to render binding, despite the lack of consideration, "promises intended to be binding, intended to be acted upon, and in fact acted upon". (Per Denning J.)

The doctrine may be relied upon provided certain conditions are satisfied:

(1) There must be an existing legal relationship between the parties—Robin and the bank are parties to a loan agreement.

(2) The promisor must have made a clear and unequivocal promise not to insist on strict legal rights—the bank has promised to write off the remainder of the debt.

(3) The promisee must have altered his position on reliance on the promise. Must the promisee have suffered some detriment as a result of reliance on the promise? Lord Denning has consistently denied this—e.g. in *W J Alan v El Nasr Co*, CA, 1972 he said all that is required is that the promisee has been "led to act differently from what he otherwise would have done".

(4) It must be inequitable for the promisor to go back on the promise. Although the presence of detriment may establish such inequity, it may be inequitable to go back on the

promise even in the absence of detriment, e.g. as in the High Trees case itself. Thus, in the case of Robin, it could be argued that it would be inequitable for the bank to insist on its strict legal rights at least without giving reasonable notice. Further, the promisee must have acted equitably. If Robin's conduct in obtaining the promise amounted to duress then it may not be inequitable for the bank to go back on its promise: *D & C Builders v Rees*, CA, 1966.

The traditional view is that the doctrine is merely suspensory (*Hughes v Metropolitan Railway*) and that the strict legal rights of the promisor can be restored on giving reasonable notice: *Tool Metal Manufacturing v Tungsten Electric Co*, HL, 1955. However, Lord Denning considered that the doctrine could extinguish rights and Lord Hodson (in *Ajayi v RT Briscoe*, PC, 1964) accepted that the promise could become "final and irrevocable" if it was impossible for the promisee to resume his position. It could further be argued that where, as here, the obligation of the debtor is to make periodic payments, the effect of "suspension" is only to allow the bank to claim instalments falling due after the expiry of the requisite period of reasonable notice, but not to claim any arrears. OTD—normally the performance of an existing contractual duty owed to the promisor does not constitute good consideration—*Stilk v Myrick*, 1809. If "pulling out all the stops" could be construed as exceeding the existing contractual duty of OTD, Robin's promise of a bonus may be enforceable—*Hartley v Ponsonby*, 1857. However, this is dubious given the strict contractual obligation of OTD to complete by December 1. Nevertheless, in *Williams v Roffey Bros*, CA 1990, it was held that the performance of an existing contractual duty could, in the absence of duress, amount to good consideration if a practical benefit is conferred on the promisor. In this case it could be argued that Robin has received the practical, as opposed to legal, benefit of the pool being completed on time. It should be noted, however, that unlike in *Williams*, here it is the promisor Robin who is approached by the promisee OTD.

Employees—on the authority of the Privy Council in *N. Z. Shipping Co Ltd v A. M. Satterthwaite Co Ltd*, PC, 1975 it would seem that the performance of an existing contractual duty already owed to a third party can be good consideration despite the absence of additional detriment. Consideration is provided by the acceptance of additional liability. On this basis, the employees would be contractually entitled to the bonus from Robin.

Question 3

Harriet, who regularly travels by bus, took her suitcase to be deposited at the left luggage office of the North Midland Bus Company. She was handed a small slip of paper which she was told by the attendant was to enable her to reclaim her suitcase. Harriet put the slip of paper in her handbag without glancing at it. On the paper appeared the following words: "The liability of the company for loss of or damage to goods deposited is limited to £50 or the value of the said goods, whichever the lower."

These words also appeared on a notice above the left luggage office counter. Harriet's suitcase contained a fur coat worth £500. When she returned to collect the suitcase the attendant informed her that it was missing and could not be found. Advise Harriet.

Answer

If Harriet is to recover full compensation from the bus company, it has to be shown that the limitation clause cannot be relied on by the company. The courts have developed a number of weapons to use against clauses excluding or restricting liability, and in addition the Unfair Contract Terms Act 1977 may require the clause to satisfy the requirement of reasonableness. The Unfair Terms in Consumer Contracts Regulations 1999 may also apply.

The first question that must be asked here is whether the limitation clause is incorporated into the contract? The courts require such a clause to be contained in a contractual document, i.e. a document which the reasonable person would expect to contain contractual terms; *Chapelton v Barry U.D.C.*, CA, 1940. On the facts given, it may be doubted whether one would expect to find contractual terms on the slip of paper handed to Harriet.

A further requirement is that reasonable and sufficient notice of the clause must be given before or at the time of the contract; *Olley v Marlborough Court*, CA, 1949. It may be that the notice over the counter, if sufficiently prominent, will serve this purpose. Further, even if there has been insufficient notice on this occasion, Harriet might be bound by a consistent course of previous dealings; *Spurling v Bradshaw*, CA, 1956. It is stated that she "regularly travels by bus". If she has travelled with this company and deposited luggage on a significant number of occasions in the past she may be bound by the clause.

Even if the clause is incorporated under the above rules, the court will apply certain rules of construction to see whether the clause clearly and unambiguously covers the breach which has taken place. Under the contra proferentem rule, the clause will be construed as narrowly as possible against the party who has inserted it and purports to rely on it. In particular, very clear words are required to exclude or restrict liability for negligence. Here, there is no express reference to negligence and in such a case the court may ask whether there is any other head of liability the words could cover; *White v John Warwick Co Ltd*, CA, 1953. In that case, general words of exclusion were held not to apply to negligence since the defendants were also under strict liability for breach of contract. However, in *Alderslade v Hendon Laundry Ltd*, CA, 1945, handkerchiefs were sent for laundering under a limitation clause referring merely to loss or damage. The clause was held to apply since if it did not apply to negligence it would lack subject-matter since there was no other head of liability to which it could possibly refer. In that case, the safekeeping of the goods was an ancillary obligation under the contract, whereas in the question it is the very purpose of the contract itself. Since it is not clear how the suitcase has been lost (e.g. negligence or deliberate misdelivery), the court may conclude the clause to be insufficiently clear to limit liability for the loss of the suitcase. Support for this view is to be found in *Woolmer v Delmer Price Ltd* (1955), although that case involved a total exclusion clause rather than a limitation clause. Finally, on construction, it is clear that the courts now view limitation clauses less strictly than exclusion clause and the House of Lords has held that the rules of construction should not be applied to limitation clauses with the same rigour as exclusion clauses; *Ailsa Craig Fishing Co v Malvern Fishing Co*, HL, 1983.

The contract is subject to the Unfair Contract Terms Act 1977 and as such the clause must satisfy the requirement of reasonableness in s.11 of the Act. The test is that the term shall have been a fair and reasonable one to be included, having regard to all the circumstances known or contemplated or which ought reasonably to have been known or contemplated by the parties when the contract was made. In the case of limitation clauses, the court must look at the resources which could be expected to be available to meet the liability and the extent to which insurance cover was open (s.11(4)). In addition, certain guidelines are laid down by Sch. 2 to the Act which may well be referred to, although strictly they are intended for sale of goods and hire-purchase contracts. It is possible to argue that the clause in this case is reasonable as the company has no means of knowing what valuables may be inside suitcases deposited with them. In the circumstances, it might not be reasonable for the risk of insurance to lie with the bus company. Thus, Harriet would be advised to attempt to avoid the clause by the tests of incorporation and construction.

Another approach may be for Harriet to argue that the clause be struck down as an unfair term under the Unfair Terms in Consumer Contracts Regulations 1999. The term clearly falls within the scope of the Regulations and she would have to argue a "significant imbalance" under Regulation 5(1). Such an argument may not succeed for the reasons set out in the previous paragraph.

Question 4

George owned a painting which he believed to be a reproduction of a work by Sergeant, the famous English water-colourist. He sold the painting to Harry, who also believed it to be a reproduction, for £80.

Harry, having consulted an expert after acquiring the painting, discovered that the painting was a genuine original work by Sergeant. Harry intended to sell it to a London dealer, Ian. After a telephone conversation with Ian concerning the merits of the painting, Harry sent it to him with a letter offering to sell it. Unfortunately, the price quoted in the letter was £80 instead of £800 (the true value of the picture). Harry's secretary had inadvertently omitted a nought. Ian sent Harry a cheque for £80 and now refuses to return the painting to him.

George, having now discovered that the painting is genuine, wishes to recover it.

Discuss the legal position of the parties.

Answer

George's only chance of recovering the painting would depend upon showing that the contract between himself and Harry is void for mistake.

This, however, is unlikely. Although a contract may be void for a common mistake where the mistake relates to the existence of the subject-matter or some fundamental fact underlying the contract, where the mistake relates to the quality of the subject-matter, there is authority that the contract is valid, even if the mistake is fundamental; *Bell v Lever Bros Ltd*, HL, 1932. In that case, Lord Atkin said, *obiter*, that if A buys a picture from B and both A and B believe the work to be that of an old master and a high price is paid, if it turns out to be a modern copy, A has no remedy, in the absence of representation or warranty. This dictum was effectively followed in *Leaf v International Galleries*, CA, 1950 where the court refused to hold void a contract for the sale of a picture where both buyer and seller mistakenly believed it had been painted by Constable.

Despite these authorities, it might be worth arguing that the parties have contracted for something fundamentally different from what they believed and therefore the contract is void. The authority for such an argument is slender; in *Nicholson and Venn v Smith Marriott* (1947), the defendants put up for auction table napkins described as having belonged to Charles I. On the faith of this description, the plaintiff bought them but they turned out to be Georgian and worth much less than the plaintiff paid for them. The buyer recovered damages for breach of contract but Hallet J. said, *obiter*, that the contract could have been treated as void for mistake. An American case, *Sherwood v Walker* (1887) is strikingly similar to the present case. The defendants sold the plaintiffs a cow. It was accepted by the majority of the court that both parties believed her to be barren but in fact she was in calf and worth about ten times what the plaintiffs paid for her. The contract was held invalid on the ground that the mistake was not merely as to the quality of the animal, but as to the very nature of the thing. On balance, however, it seems that if the tenor of these authorities were to be followed it would be a novel departure from the accepted view concerning mistake as to quality. In the absence of operative mistake, George might be able to recover damages if Harry had warranted or represented that the painting was a Sergeant. Rescission for misrepresentation here could only be ordered if the contract between Harry and Ian is also void. This is discussed below.

Turning to the contract between Harry and Ian, Harry may be able to obtain an order of rescission in equity on the ground of operative unilateral mistake. A contract will be void for unilateral mistake where the mistake is as to the terms of the contract and the other party is, or must be taken to be, aware of the mistake; *Hartog v Colin and Shields* (1939). Here, because of the prior telephone call, it is likely that Ian is well aware of the true value of the painting and therefore must be taken to know that the sum stated in the offer is a mistake. In *Webster v Cecil* (1861), the parties were negotiating the sale of some property and the vendor wrote to the purchaser offering £1,250 instead of £2,250. It was held that since the vendor had already refused to sell for £2,000, the purchaser must have been aware of the mistake and specific performance was refused.

Question 5

Millicent owns a factory manufacturing clothing. In January, the heating system of the factory broke down and she was forced to lay off the work-force. Millicent engaged Fixit Ltd to repair the system. They agreed to complete the necessary work within one week.

Owing to supply problems, the work was not completed within the week and Fixit offered to install a temporary system which would enable half-day working at the factory. Millicent rejected this offer. In the event, the repair work took two months and as a result Millicent lost a highly remunerative contract to supply knitwear to the armed forces. Millicent is now claiming a total of £8,000 by way of lost profits.

Advise Fixit Ltd as to their liability in damages.

Further, consider the position if the contract between Millicent and Fixit referred to above had contained the following provision: "If the repair work is not completed within one week, Fixit shall pay Millicent, by way of agreed damages, the sum of £5,000 plus £2,000 for every week during which the work is unfinished."

Answer

Fixit are in breach of contract and the first issue to be considered is the extent of their liability. Millicent is claiming a total of £8,000 by way of lost profits and it may be that some of that loss is too remote.

The test of remoteness for damages in breach of contract was originally laid down in *Hadley v Baxendale* (1854) and refined in subsequent cases, notably *The Heron II*, HL, 1969. The position is that the plaintiff may recover for such loss as arises naturally out of the breach, i.e. according to the usual course of things as the probable result of the breach, or, in the case of special or unusual loss, if the loss could reasonably be supposed to have been within the contemplation of the parties, at the time of the contract, as the probable result of the breach.

Applying these principles to the facts in question, it is clear that Fixit must have envisaged loss of normal business profits, but whether they should be liable for the loss of the "highly remunerative" contract may depend on the state of their knowledge at the time of the contract. It is possible that this loss is too remote. In *Victoria Laundry (Windsor) Ltd v Newman Industries Ltd*, CA, 1949, the defendants agreed to sell the plaintiffs a boiler. The defendants knew it was required for the plaintiffs' immediate use in their business of launderers and dyers. Delivery was five months late in breach of contract by the defendants. The plaintiffs claimed loss of profits; (i) £16 per week representing the loss of "normal" new business they would have taken on; and (ii) £262 per week which they could have earned under lucrative dyeing contracts with the Ministry of Supply. The Court of Appeal held that the defendants' knowledge was such as to render them liable for (i), but not (ii) about which they knew nothing.

Further, there is a duty on the plaintiff to mitigate his loss, i.e. he cannot recover in respect of loss that could reasonably have been avoided; *British Westinghouse Co v Underground Electric Railway Co*, HL, 1912. Here, Fixit have offered to install a temporary heating system and Millicent has rejected the offer and so the question may turn on whether this refusal was reasonable in the circumstances. The burden of proving the failure to mitigate will lie on Fixit.

If the contract had contained the provision referred to in the last paragraph of the question, the court would have to consider the nature of the provision. If the provision can be regarded as a genuine pre-estimate of the loss (a liquidated or agreed damages clause), the plaintiff will be able to recover the sum stipulated without proof of loss. Alternatively, if it is held to be in the nature of a threat to compel the other party to perform (a penalty), the provision will be invalid and the plaintiff may recover only for the loss he has actually suffered.

Guidelines for distinguishing between liquidated damages and penalty were laid down by the House of Lords in *Dunlop Pneumatic Tyre Co Ltd v New Garage and Motor Co Ltd*, HL, 1915, some of which may be relevant here. Thus, the fact that the provision is referred to as "agreed damages" will not prevent it being a penalty if that is its true nature. In particular, if the sum is extravagant and unconscionable in comparison with the greatest loss which could conceivably follow the breach, the sum may be regarded as a penalty.

In the question, Millicent's claim for damages (including items that may be too remote) amounts to £8,000, whereas under the provision in the contract, after eight weeks' delay, some £19,000 would be payable. In view of this it is arguable that the provision is in the nature of a penalty and not recoverable. Millicent would be entitled to recover for her actual loss.

INDEX

[all references are to page number]